W. Blumer, William Nicoll

Antiquities of Ionia

W. Blumer, William Nicoll

Antiquities of Ionia

ISBN/EAN: 9783742846648

Manufactured in Europe, USA, Canada, Australia, Japa

Cover: Foto ©ninafisch / pixelio.de

Manufactured and distributed by brebook publishing software (www.brebook.com)

W. Blumer, William Nicoll

Antiquities of Ionia

ANTIQUITIES

OF

IONIA,

PUBLISHED BY THE SOCIETY

OF

DILETTANTI.

PART THE FIRST.

LONDON:

PRINTED BY W. BULMER AND W. NICOL.
SOLD BY G. AND W. NICOL, BOOKSELLERS TO HIS MAJESTY;
PAYNE AND FOSS, PALL-MALL; LONGMAN AND CO. PATERNOSTER-ROW; AND
RODWELL AND MARTIN, BOND STREET.

MDCCCXXI.

MEMBERS OF THE SOCIETY.

MDCCLXIX.

IN THE ORDER OF THEIR SENIORITY

Lord le DESPENCER.
Sir JAMES GRAY.
Lord HYDE.
Mr. BOONE.
Major General GRAY.
Mr. HOWE.
Mr. FAUQUIER.
Earl of BESSBOROUGH.
Earl of SANDWICH.
Right Hon. Mr. ELLIS.
Duke of BEDFORD.
Mr. BOYLE.
Mr. DINGLEY.
Mr. STUART.
Mr. REVETT.
Earl of CHARLEMONT.
Lord STOPFORD.
Sir THOMAS ROBINSON.
Sir EDWARD DERING.
Mr. PHELPS.
Hon. Mr. ROBINSON.
Mr. WOOD.
Mr. MACKYE ROSS.
Mr. DUNDAS.
Colonel CARLETON.
Marquis of MOUNTHERMOR.
Mr. CROWLE.

Earl of CLANBRASSIL.
Mr. PENNANT.
Mr. BRAND.
Mr. CREWE.
Hon. Lieut. Col. St. JOHN.
Duke of ROXBOROUGH.
Earl of BELLAMONT.
Duke of MARLBOROUGH.
Earl SPENCER.
Viscount PALMERSTON.
Mr. SOUTHWELL.
Hon. Lieut. Col. NUGENT.
Mr. SCRAFTON.
Earl of UPPER OSSORY.
Mr. WEDDEL.
Mr. REYNOLDS.
Viscount FORTROSE.
Duke of BUCCLEUGH.
Mr. FITZGERALD.
Earl of CARLISLE.
Sir SAMPSON GIDEON.
Earl FITZWILLIAM.
Hon. Mr. CHARLES FOX.
Hon. Mr. HOBART.
Mr. MYTTON.
Lord SYDNEY.
Mr. GREGORY.

SOCIETY OF DILETTANTI.

AN. SOC. LXXXIX.

RICHARD PAYNE KNIGHT, Esq.
Sir HENRY C. ENGLEFIELD, Bart.
ROGER WILBRAHAM, Esq.
JAMES DAWKINS, Esq.
WILLIAM MITFORD, Esq.
The Earl of GUILFORD.
The Earl of HARDWICKE.
The Lord DUNDAS.
Sir THOMAS LAWRENCE.
WILLIAM SOTHEBY, Esq.
JOHN SYMMONS, Esq.
Hon. WILLIAM R. SPENCER.
JOHN HAWKINS, Esq.
JOHN B. S. MORRITT, Esq.
The Duke of SOMERSET.
Right Hon. Sir W. DRUMMOND, K. C.
THOMAS HOPE, Esq.
The Lord NORTHWICK.
The Duke of HAMILTON.
Sir JOHN COX HIPPISLEY, Bart.
The Viscount MORPETH.
The Earl COWPER.
The Earl MORLEY.
CHARLES W. WYNNE, Esq.
SAMUEL ROGERS, Esq.
Right Hon. R. POLE CAREW.
The Earl of ABERDEEN.
Sir WATKIN W. WYNNE, Bart.
HENRY PHILIP HOPE, Esq.
Sir WILLIAM GELL.

The Earl of CHARLEVILLE.
WILLIAM DICKENSON, Esq.
FREDERICK FOSTER, Esq.
WILLIAM WILKINS, Esq.
WILLIAM HAMILTON, Esq.
The Earl of DUNMORE.
FOSTER CUNLIFFE, Esq.
PEREGRINE TOWNELEY, Esq.
WILLIAM FITZHUGH, Esq.
EDWARD DAVENPORT, Esq.
Colonel LEAKE.
The Earl of SURREY.
RICHARD HEBER, Esq.
Right Hon. JOHN H. FRERE.
The Marquis of STAFFORD.
The Marquis of LANSDOWNE.
The Earl of CHARLEMONT.
THOMAS LEGH, Esq.
RICHARD WESTMACOTT, Esq.
The Earl of ROSEBERY.
H. GALLY KNIGHT, Esq.
NICHOLAS FAZAKERLY, Esq.
HENRY HALLAM, Esq.
Hon. T. DUNDAS.
The Duke of BEDFORD.
Hon. R. H. CLIVE.
Hon. WILLIAM PONSONBY.
Hon. GEORGE JAMES ELLIS.
WILLIAM BANKES, ESQ.

JUNE 1. MDCCCXXI.

PREFACE TO THE FIRST EDITION.

In the variety of literary productions which are ushered into the world by a Preface to the reader, there is no species to which that kind of introduction seems more necessary than to that which, consisting rather of matters of *fact* than *opinion*, derives its merit more from the writer's veracity than from his talents for composition. A work of genius speaks for itself; in such case apology is idle, and justification superfluous: but the traveller who commences author on the humbler pretensions of a plain and faithful relation of what he has seen, whose candour and accuracy are more at stake than his taste or judgment, cannot more effectually recommend himself to public favour than by a fair account of the opportunities he had of being informed, the means by which he acquired his knowledge, and the manner in which he collected his facts. The reader of real curiosity will expect some explanation of this kind, in order to judge what credit this work may deserve; and the following short narrative is intended to satisfy so reasonable an expectation.

In the year 1734, some gentlemen who had travelled in Italy, desirous of encouraging, *at home*, a taste for those objects which had contributed so much to their entertainment *abroad*, formed themselves into a Society, under the name of the *DILETTANTI*, and agreed upon such regulations as they thought necessary to keep up the spirit of their scheme.

PREFACE TO THE FIRST EDITION.

As this narrative professes the strictest regard to truth, it would be disingenuous to insinuate, that a serious plan for the promotion of Arts was the only motive for forming this Society: friendly and social intercourse was, undoubtedly, the first great object in view; but while, in this respect, no set of men ever kept up more religiously to their original institution, it is hoped this work will show that they have not, for that reason, abandoned the cause of virtù, in which they are also engaged, or forfeited their pretensions to that character which is implied in the name they have assumed.

Upon a report of the state of the Society's finances in the year 1764, it appeared that they were possessed of a considerable sum above what their current services required. Various schemes were proposed for applying part of this money to some purpose which might promote taste, and do honour to the Society; and after some consideration it was resolved, " That a person or persons properly qualified should be sent, with sufficient appointments, to certain parts of the East, to collect informations relative to the former state of those countries, and particularly to procure exact descriptions of the ruins of such monuments of antiquity as are yet to be seen in those parts."

Three persons were elected for this undertaking. Mr. Chandler, of Magdalen College, Oxford, editor of the *Marmora Oxoniensia*, was appointed to execute the classical part of the plan. The province of architecture was assigned to Mr. Revett, who had already given a satisfactory specimen of his accuracy and diligence, in his measures of the remains of antiquity at Athens. The choice of a proper person for taking views, and copying bas-reliefs, fell upon Mr. Pars, a young painter of promising talents. A committee was appointed to fix their salaries, and draw up their instructions; in which, at the same time that the different objects of their respective departments were distinctly pointed out, they were all strictly enjoined to keep a regular journal, and hold a constant correspondence with the Society.

They embarked, on the ninth of June, 1764, in the Anglicana, Captain Stewart, bound for Constantinople, and were put on shore at the Dardanelles on the twenty-fifth of August. Having visited the Sigean Promontory, the Ruins of Troas, with the Islands of Tenedos and Scio, they arrived at Smyrna on the eleventh of September. From that city, as their head-quarters, they made several excursions. On the twentieth of August, 1765, they sailed from Smyrna, and arrived at Athens on the thirty-first of the same month, touching at Sunium and Ægina in their way. They staid at Athens till the eleventh of June, 1766, visiting Marathon, Eleusis, Salamis, Megara, and other places in the neighbourhood. Leaving Athens, they proceeded, by the little Island of Calauria, to Trœzene, Epidaurus, Argos, and Corinth. From this they visited Delphi, Patræ, Elis, and Zante, whence they sailed, on the thirty-first of August, in the Diligence brig, Captain Long, bound for Bristol, and arrived in England the second of November following.

The materials which they brought home were thought not unworthy of the Public: the Society therefore directed them to give a specimen of their labours out of what they had found most worthy of observation in Ionia; a country in many respects curious, and perhaps, after Attica, the most deserving the attention of a classical traveller. Athens, it is true, having had the good fortune to possess more original genius than ever was collected in so narrow a compass, at one period, reaped the fruits of literary competition in a degree that never fell to the lot of any other people, and has been generally allowed to fix the æra which has done most honour to science, and to take the lead among the ancient Greek Republics in matters of taste: however, it is much to be doubted, whether, upon a fair enquiry into the rise and progress of Letters and Arts, they do not, upon the whole, owe as much to Ionia, and the adjoining coast, as to any country of antiquity. The knowledge of Nature was first taught in the Ionic school: and as Geometry, Astronomy, and other branches of the Mathematics, were cultivated here sooner than in other parts of Greece, it is not extraordinary that the first Greek navigators, who passed the Pillars of Hercules, and extended their commerce to the ocean, should have been Ionians. Here History had its birth, and here it acquired a considerable degree of perfection. The first writer, who reduced the knowledge of Medicine, or the means of preserving health, to an Art, was of this neighbourhood: and here the Father of Poetry produced a standard for composition, which no age or country has dared to depart from, or has been able to surpass. But Architecture belongs more particularly to this country than to any other; and of the three Greek Orders it seems justly entitled to the honour of having invented the two first, though one of them only bears its name; for though the temple of Juno at Argos suggested the general idea of what was after called the Doric, its proportions were first established here. As to the other Arts, which also depend upon Design, they have flourished no where more than in Ionia; nor has any spot of the same extent produced more painters and sculptors of distinguished talents.

Among the remains of antiquity which have hitherto escaped the injuries of time, there are none in which our curiosity is more interested, than the ruins of those buildings which were distinguished by Vitruvius, and other ancient writers, for their elegance and magnificence. Such are the temple of Bacchus at Teos, the country of Anacreon; the temple dedicated to Minerva, at Priene, by Alexander of Macedon; and the famous temple of Apollo Didymæus, near Miletus. However mutilated and decayed these buildings now are, yet surely every fragment is valuable, which preserves, in some degree, the ideas of symmetry and proportion which prevailed at that happy period of taste.

Thus far the Society have thought proper, both in justice to the public, and to the authors of the following work, to give a short account of the original occasion of the undertaking, and of the manner in which it has been hitherto conducted. They have directed the plates of this specimen to be engraved at their expense, in hopes that it may encourage the Editors to proceed upon the remaining materials of their voyage, which will be put into their hands with that view.

INTRODUCTION.

The Society of Dilettanti being convinced by a former survey of the shores of Asia Minor made, at their expense, with the view of searching for the remains of ancient architecture, that much of that interesting quarter of the globe contained monuments of antiquity hitherto unnoticed or imperfectly described, had long contemplated a second mission, provided with more ample means and more extensive powers. Accordingly, in October of the year 1812, Mr., now Sir William, Gell, accompanied by two architects, Mr. John Peter Gandy and Mr. Francis Bedford, embarked for the Mediterranean, having received the necessary instructions for the mode of their proceeding.

The result of their researches in Attica has been made known by the splendid work which was published from the drawings transmitted to the Society. In the present work, and in another now in progress, it is proposed to give to the public the remains of ancient architecture which still exist to attest the former splendour of the Ionian colonies of Greece.

At the period when the first work of the Society appeared, Grecian architecture was very little understood; for, although the first volume of the Antiquities of Athens had been seven years before the public, yet this portion of this justly celebrated work referred only to buildings of little note, compared with the nobler productions of the Athenians, and those of very simple construction.

Many of the architectural details of the buildings selected for publication in the first volume of Ionian Antiquities, where they differed from the better known specimens of Roman art, were disregarded by the artists attached to the first mission; and several omissions, the consequence of their more limited means of excavation and inspection, necessarily occurred.

The attention of the later mission was, in the first instance, directed to the correction of the errors which had arisen from the imperfect knowledge of Grecian architecture; and to examine with greater minuteness, by means of excavations made within and around the buildings, the plans and mode of construction observed in the edifices which formed the subject of the first volume of Ionian Antiquities.

The researches for this purpose, which were conducted with great science and ability, have put the Society in possession of more ample documents, both in general and in detail, relating to the buildings in question; and have enabled them to re-publish the first volume of the Antiquities of Ionia, which has been long out of print, corrected and considerably augmented.

Amongst the additions to our architectural knowledge which the recent publication on Attica has been instrumental in disseminating, one of the most interesting is the mode, by means of which the Greek architects were enabled to cover their temples in such a manner as to exclude the wet, without departing from that depression of the roof, which is one amongst many of the characteristics of Grecian architecture. This has been so fully illustrated, as to leave nothing further to be desired on the subject

The frame-work of timber which supported this elegant covering had, of course, long ceased to exist; but as the art of carpentry is now much more advanced than at the period of their construction, we have little to regret on this occasion. Of the ancient mode of ornamenting cielings we have ample means of judging. Where the span was small, as in the porticoes and ambulatories around the temples, the *lacunaria* were stone or marble. The buildings of Athens furnish us with examples wherein beams of those lasting materials, supported by walls and columns, formed the ornamental ceiling below the timbers of the roof. But the labours of the mission directed to this end have made known the principles on which this practice has been carried to a much greater extent, by the complete restoration of the marble ceiling of the Eleusinian Propylæa. These discoveries, whilst they exhibit proofs of the great skill of the Grecian architects, enable us to appreciate the labour and cost incurred in covering temples of considerable extent; and thus explain why such buildings as the temple of Jupiter Olympius at Agrigentum, and of Apollo Didymaeus, remained unfinished, when so little appeared, on a first view of the subject, wanting to their completion.

It is not, however, to be supposed, that temples of any considerable span would admit of a similar mode of covering; but there is every reason to believe, that timber was here employed to answer a similar purpose; where the kind of ornament might be retained, although the material was necessarily different. Certain it is, that some temples were embellished with ornamental ceilings below the frame-work of timber, which supported the tiles. A passage in Pausanias is decisive as to this practice. In the account of the Heræum at Olympia, he states, upon the authority of Aristarchus, that when the roof was repaired, the body of a man in armour was found lying in the interval between the roof, constructed for the support of the tiles, and the ceiling introduced for the sake of ornament.*

The same causes which have obliged us to deduce from analogy the method of construction observed in ornamental ceilings, have enveloped, in almost total obscurity, a subject of some interest connected with the religious observances of

---

* Ητεαξύ αυτοτέρου οροφθαι και τε ις εκπείναι στέγει, και τε διηρφοτε Παυσανιας. v. 20.

the ancients. None of the discoveries of modern times have thrown light upon the real or supposed practice of leaving a portion of the cella exposed to the sky, in temples termed, by Vitruvius, Hypæthral.

This peculiarity of construction is alluded to by no other author: all the notices of ancient writers lead to the direct inference of a contrary custom. M. Quatremere de Quincy, in a very elaborate essay published in the Mémoires of the French Institute,[*] has entered into a learned disquisition on this subject, and brought together a number of passages from ancient authors bearing upon this question.

The learned antiquary, however, sets out with assuming it to be absolutely necessary that the temples of the Greeks should have admitted, by some expedient or other, the light of heaven; in direct contradiction to the inference to be deduced from Vitruvius, who is altogether silent on the subject of windows, and only pretends that light was admitted through an opening left in the roof of temples of a certain class.

The concurrent testimony of ancient writers leads, as we have already observed, to the supposition that the introduction of artificial light alone was considered by the nations of antiquity as more consonant to the spirit of their theology; where much depended upon pomp and pageantry. In the celebration of the mystic ceremonies of Eleusis the sudden transition from the outer darkness to the brilliant display of the illuminated interior, is described as producing the strongest sensations of awe and astonishment.

It is not to be denied that we have some few examples of Roman temples where light was admitted by means of windows;[†] but these were of rare occurrence, and only met with in buildings of little note, such as the temple of Fortuna-Virilis, and the two circular temples of Vesta at Rome and Tivoli. Amongst the remains of Grecian architecture, there is nothing to confirm the conjecture

---

[*] Classe d'histoire et de litterature ancienne, tom. iii

[†] The temple of Minerva-Pandrosus at Athens has three windows in the western front, intended to light a passage or pronaos, where it is conjectured the sacred olive tree grew and was preserved.

that windows were ever introduced for the purpose of affording light to the interior of temples.

The only positive proof of the existence of temples constructed with an aperture in the roof, is derived from the assertion of Vitruvius, in a passage devoted to the description of hypæthral temples: "Hypæthros vero decastylos est in pronao et postico. Reliqua omnia eadem habet, quæ dipteros, sed interiore parte columnas in altitudine duplices remotas a parietibus ad circuitionem ut porticus peristyliorum. Medium autem sub divo est sine tecto, aditusque valvarum ex utraque parte in pronao et postico. Hujus autem exemplar Romæ non est, sed Athenis, in Asty, Jovis templo Olympii."*

Rome, rich as it was in temples, offering no example in illustration of this mode of construction, Vitruvius, who had obtained some knowledge of Grecian buildings from the works of Greek architects, refers his readers to the temple of Jupiter-Olympius, at Athens. This magnificent structure indisputably possessed two of the characters requisite in hypæthral temples—it was decastyle and dipteral: we must therefore conclude it was not wanting in the third; and consequently that the middle division of the cella was open to the sky.

This passage, as we have already observed, is the only authority we have for the observance of such a mode of construction; and coming from a professed architect, it must be considered conclusive. But in proportion to the weight which is attached to such authority must be the objection to any departure from the position he maintains. If, therefore, we are compelled to allow that hypæthral temples existed, we must also admit that they were both decastyle and dipteral; and that the introduction of columns within the cella alone does not constitute an hypæthral temple: and further, that a non-conformity with *either* of the two concomitant requisites, is an insuperable objection to any hypothesis of a contrary tendency.

* Civil Architecture of Vitruvius, p. 10.
We have adopted a recent reading of the latter part of this passage which, by a simple correction, restores its sense and consistency. It is singular enough that Casaubon, without offering any correction of the text, interprets the passage in the proper sense. "Sane Vitruvius testatur est. templum Jovis Olympii quod erat Athenis [nam et ibi fuit] hypæthrum fuisse et sine tecto." *Ad Strab.* viii.

Where then, we ask, is the authority for assuming the Parthenon at Athens, the temple of Jupiter at Olympia, and the temples of Pæstum and Egina to have been hypæthral? No such authority exists; and the speculations of Stuart and those who have followed him, originating in error, rest upon conjecture only.*

Some temples are described by ancient authors as remaining without a roof, from accidental causes; such, for instance, as the temple of Apollo-Didymæus, one of the subjects of the following work. Strabo informs us that the greatness of its span was the obstacle to its completion, and not that it was part of the original design.†

One of the most celebrated temples of antiquity, the temple of Jupiter at Olympia, we are informed by Pausanias, had its cella in three divisions, made by a row of columns along the walls on each side. This building we know to have been an hexastyle temple; of course it could not be dipteral. If, therefore, any weight be due to the authority of Vitruvius, this temple was not hypæthral. This conclusion is confirmed by a passage in Strabo,‡ who in speaking of the chryselephantine statue of Jupiter, observes, it was colossal, and so nearly touching the highest part of the cieling, that if it were to rise it would destroy the roof. As this proof of the existence of a roof over the centre division of the cella destroys all notions of an hypæthral temple, M. Quatremere de Quincy is obliged to have recourse to another hypothesis, and supposes that the

---

* One of the weakest points in the argument used by Stuart is the conjecture that the parapetasma exhibited in the celebration of the Panathenaic festival, was employed in the protection of the statue exposed, as he imagined, in the open area of the cella. This splendid piece of tapestry was probably suspended before the entrance: a similar custom is prevalent throughout the east at this day. The parapetasma was hung before the entrance into every Egyptian temple; and Pausanias informs us, that in the temple of Jupiter at Olympia, and in the temple at Ephesus, this curtain was let fall from the cieling to the pavement, contrary to the usual mode of drawing it up. The use, therefore, of the parapetasma and its mode of suspension are obvious.

† Strabo, xiv. 634.

‡ Μέγεθος δὲ τοιοῦτον ἐτύχε τὸ ξόανον ἔχειν ὥστε (sic in MSS.) καίπερ τοῦ ναοῦ μεγίστου ὄντος, δοκεῖν ἀστοχῆσαι τῆς συμμετρίας τὸν τεχνίτην, καθήμενον πεποιηκότα, ἁπτόμενον δὲ σχεδόν τι τῇ κορυφῇ τῆς ὀροφῆς ὥστ᾽ ἔμφασιν ποιεῖν, ἐὰν ὀρθὸς γένηται διαναστὰς ἀποστεγάσειν τὸν ναόν. Strabo, viii. 353.

M. de Quincy interprets this passage to favour his own hypothesis on the vaulted cielings of temples: but if the form of the cieling is intended to be designated by the word ὀροφή, it must mean pedimental-shaped, like the roof, made by two straight lines inclined to each other, and forming an obtuse angle.

cielings of ancient temples were vaulted and furnished with sky-lights, *jours en comble*. It would be needless to follow this industrious and ingenious writer throughout his long treatise; it will be sufficient to shew how totally he has misconstrued his authorities in one or two instances.

In a recent publication of the Society, the mystic temple of Ceres at Eleusis has been described, both from the remains and from ancient authorities. It is evident, from the fragments of shafts found within the cella, that Plutarch's description of interior columns is correct. And as the introduction of interior columns constitutes an hypæthral temple in the opinion of our author, this magnificent edifice is brought forward in support of his hypothesis. In speaking of this temple Plutarch records the names of those artists who contributed to its completion; and amongst others he mentions that of Xenocles, whose merit consisted in covering a certain portion, or perhaps the whole, of the temple with a pediment roof— τὸ δὲ ὀπαῖον ἐπὶ τοῦ ἀνακτόρου Ξενοκλῆς ὁ Χολαργεὺς ἐκορύφωσε. The literal meaning of this passage is so obvious, that the construction of M. de Quincy is perfectly inadmissible.*

As an additional proof of an opening in the roof of temples, M. de Quincy relates a dramatic representation, in allusion to the Eleusinian mysteries, described by Lucian in his life of the pretended prophet Alexander, which took place in a temple dedicated to Glycon. The temple being arranged in the manner of a theatre,† Alexander, who represents Endymion, lies down upon the stage, when a certain Rutilia, personating Luna, *descends from the cieling*, as if from heaven.‡ From this recital M. de Quincy concludes that the roof was perforated. But why, in the dramatic representation thus described, it follows that the temple must be hypæthral, is no more obvious, than that the same exposure to the sky is necessary in similar representations upon the French stage.

In support of his opinion, that the roofs of temples were vaulted, our author quotes the description, by Pausanias, of the temple of Apollo-Epicurius at

---

* Le mot κορυφὴ veut dire en Grec, *sommet, faîte, faîtage,* fastigium: κορυφόω en use *fastigiare forniceo*, signifie par conséquent, *pratiquer une ouverture dans le faîtage*. See the "Unedited Antiquities of Attica." c. iv. p. 31.
† Ἧκε γάρ τις τῶν ἐξίσημα, ὡς ἐκ τινος παρασκευῆς. Lucian, Pseudom. 19.
‡ Κατῄει δὲ τις ἄνω τις τις ὀροφῆς, ὡς ἐξ οὐρανοῦ, αὐτῷ τις Σελήνη, Ῥουτίλια τις. Ibid.

Phigalia, with the construction of which we are become well acquainted from the excavations made within and around it which have enriched our national collection with some valuable specimens of Grecian art. Pausanias informs us that the roof, as well as the temple, was of marble,* a fact which has been confirmed by the discovery of some of the marble tiles, in contradistinction to the use of terra-cotta tiles in temples of minor importance. This passage is interpreted to signify a vaulted roof, constructed with stone, in opposition to the manifest meaning of the author.

A similar interpretation is given to another passage of the same author, relating to the temple of Mercury at Megalopolis,† of which nothing more was to be seen in the time of Pausanias than the χέλυς λίθος, or stone threshold of the door-way. Until we can be convinced that a vaulted roof of a temple can remain without its supporting walls, we must be permitted to give to the word χέλυς, and its synonym χελωνίς, a much more limited signification.

Having shewn that in the construction of the generality of temples, no provision was contemplated or made for the admission of light, otherwise than by the door-way, it remains that some observations should be made on the means by which the objects within the cella were rendered discernible.

The illumination of the interior of the mystic temple at Eleusis, by means of artificial light, has already been alluded to: such an expedient seems to have suited the religious notions of the Greeks; and as far as we are enabled to ascertain, was that to which they had recourse, not of necessity, but by preference and design. The golden lamp of Callimachus, which is recorded by Pausanias ‡ to have burned perpetually before the statue of the goddess in the temple of Minerva-Polias at Athens, is decisive as to the mode in which the interior of the temples in Greece were lighted. Both Thucydides§ and Pausanias‖, describe the accident that befel the ancient temple of Juno, near Mycenæ, which was destroyed by a lamp left by the priestess near some of the interior decorations.

---

* ὄροφον καὶ ἀΐστε ἔγραφε. viii. 41 ; forte scribendum sit ?, καὶ ἀΐστε καὶ ὁ ἔγραφε. Facius observes.
† Καὶ εἶδε δ᾽ οὖτσι ὅτι ἡ χέλωνη λίθος. viii. 30.
‡ i. 26. Strabo, ix. 396.   § iv. 133.   ‖ viii. 37.

INTRODUCTION.

Pausanias informs us that a fire was kept constantly burning before the ancient statue of Pan, placed in his temple at Acacesius, in Arcadia;[*] as also in the temple of Ceres and Proserpine at Mantinea. Near the Prytaneum at Elis there was likewise a small temple, where fire was constantly burning.[+]

In the forum of Pharæ there was an oracular building, on the altar of which brazen lamps were fixed; those who came to consult the oracle first burnt frankincense, and filling the lamps with oil, lighted them, then placing an offering on the altar, consulted the statue.[‡] Hence it appears that artificial light was adopted in the religious ceremonies of the Greeks, from whence the custom descended to the Romans.[§]

Pliny alludes to the use of lamps suspended in the temples of Italy;[∥] and the custom was derived from a very remote antiquity, for Plutarch mentions the perpetual lamp, of great celebrity, suspended in the temple of Jupiter Ammon.[¶] And Alexander brought from Thebes, from the temple of Apollo, the palm tree, from the branches of which lamps were suspended. The ten lamps in the temple of Solomon placed upon altars on the right and left of the cella are decisive evidence of this early custom."

---

[*] Paus. viii. 27.   [+] Ib. v. 15.   Ib. vii. 22.
[‡] A scene of Aeschylus introduces us into the presence of Minerva, and the Furies assembled within her temple at Athens, before the statue of the goddess.
Minerva dismisses the Furies with an address, which is thus rendered by Potter:

    I like these votive measures; and will send
    The bright flames of these splendour shedding torches,
    With those that guard my hallow'd image here,
    Attendant on you to the dark abodes
    Beneath the earth.   *Furies*

Hence it appears that the interior of the temple was lighted by means of torches.
[§] EXEDRIS II. CVM SVIS EXEDRVSTIS ET LUCERN. *Gruter*, Inscr.
Vidi Cupidinem argenteum cum lampade. Cic. in Verr. ii.
Placuere et Lychnuchi pensiles in delubro, xxxiv. 5.
Horace alludes to the neglected state of the temples and statues, the latter of which were suffered to remain covered with smoke, from what cause is sufficiently obvious.

    Delicta majorum immeritus lues
    Romane; donec templa refeceris,
    Aedesque labentes deorum, et
        Foeda nigro simulachra fumo.   Lib. iii. od. vi.

[¶] De orac. defect. i. 614.
" Καὶ ἔθηκε τὰς λύχνας τὰς χρυσᾶς ἕσω—Καὶ ἔθηκε ἐκ τῶ ναῶ. Par. 2. c. iv. 7.

It has been objected to the use of lamps, the inefficiency of the light in discriminating the ornaments of the interior; but this objection would be equally valid if applied to the temples and tombs of Egypt, where internal decoration has been carried to a great extent; the paintings of most brilliant colouring, with which the walls and columns are entirely covered, could only have been seen by the introduction of artificial light.

We have a further proof of the prevalence of this custom, in the existence of an office in perfect conformity with its observance. The care of the lamps devolved upon a minister of the temple, who also exercised functions which might be thought of higher pretensions. Chandler found the following inscription in the Choragic monument of Thrasyllus, which is now converted into a Greek church, and dedicated to the *Panagia Spiliotissa*, or, Our Lady of the Grotto.

    ... ΚΟΣΜΑ ΚΑΙ ΤΟ ΑΥΤΟΥΣ Υ
    ΠΕΡ ΤΑΣ ΚΙΓΚΛΙΔΑΣ ΚΑΙ ΤΗΝ
    ΦΡΟΝΤΙΔΑ ΤΗ ΘΕΟ ΕΚ
    ΤΩΝ ΙΔΙΩΝ ΑΝΕΘΗΚΕΝ Ε
    ΠΙ ΙΕΡΕΙΑΣ ΔΑ ΚΑΙ ΑΥΤΗΣ
    ΕΡΣ ΥΙΩΝ ΚΑΙ ΤΑ ΠΕΡΙ ΑΥΤΗΝ
    ΟΣΑ ΚΑΙ ΑΘΑΝΑΣΙΑΝ ΑΥ
    ΤΗΣ ΚΑΙ ΟΝΕΙΡΟΚΡΙΤΑΙ ... κ. τ. λ.*

From the foregoing authorities it is evident that the custom of lighting the interior of temples by artificial means, was of ancient origin, and of general observance. The notices of this custom by early writers are certainly of rare occurrence; but on the other hand, there are none of a contrary tendency, excepting the one of Vitruvius, previously cited, which is applicable only to decastyle temples constructed with double peristyles.

* Chandler. Inscrip. Pars 2. 55. xxix.

CONTENTS.

CHAPTER I.
Teos 1

CHAPTER II.
Priene 11

CHAPTER III.
Didyma 29

CHAPTER IV.
Labranda 53

CHAPTER V.
Samos 89

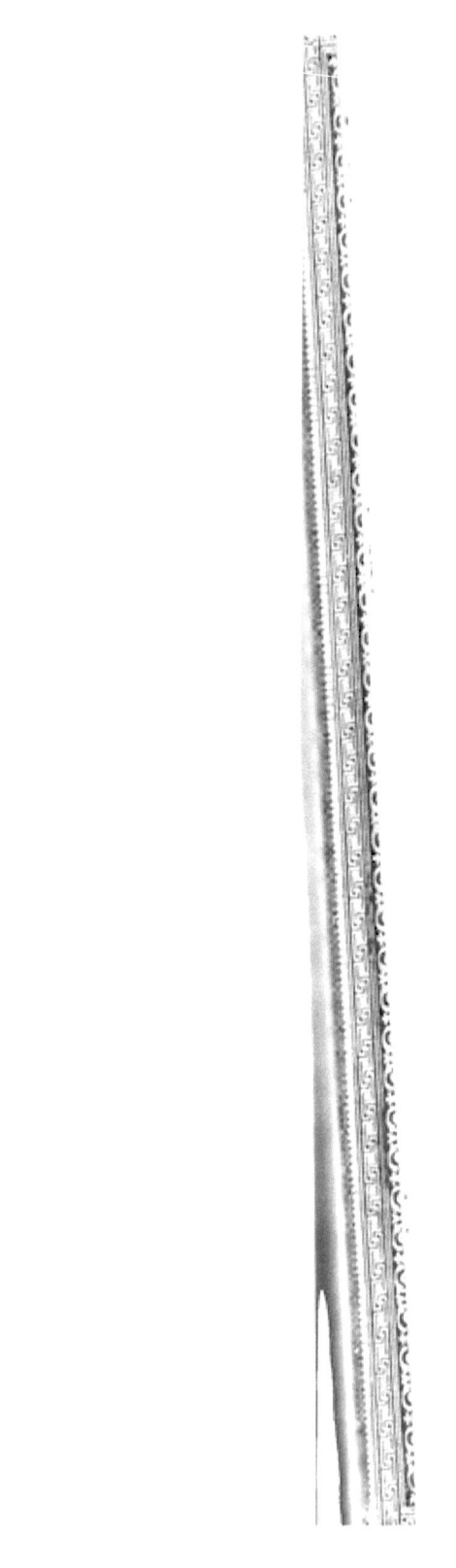

CHAPTER I.

TEOS.

AMONG the many volumes which have perished by time and accident, or been purposely destroyed, the lover of rational Architecture will particularly regret the invaluable treatises on that noble art once extant, written by masters equally eminent for genius and science, and laudably intent on shewing how both were united in the structures they had raised; by demonstrating the principles on which they proceeded; marking the propriety of the disposition, the proportion, and ornaments, they had invented or adopted; and explaining the harmony and symmetry of their design; transmitting, with the fabric, its history to future ages.

The memory of several of these ancient worthies is preserved to us by Vitruvius,* who distinguishes, in this meritorious number, the great architects of the two magnificent temples at Teos and Priene. If their dissertations yet remained, with what pleasure would the curious artist compare, correct, and supply this work! As it is, he must contemplate with concern these rich fragments, as all that can be saved from the general wreck; and, while he admires and improves, may still rejoice that the authors are not become mere names, like many in the catalogue, but at least survive thus far.

---

* Porticus Saturni de symmetriis Doricorum edidit volumen. De æde Junonis, quæ est Sami, Ionica, Theodorus. Ionica Ephesi, quæ est Dianæ, Ctesiphon et Metagenes. De fano Minervæ, quod est Prienæ, Ionicum, Pythius.— Hermogenes de æde Dianæ Ionica, quæ est Magnesiæ pseudodipteros, et Liberi patris Teo monopteros (vel peripteros). VITRUV. Præf. Lib. vii MSS.

TEOS* was situated on the south side of the isthmus of a small peninsula, which terminates on the west, in a low sharp point. It had two ports, one adjoining, and the other behind the city, distant thirty stadia; being nearly the width of the Isthmus. The latter was anciently called Geræsticus.

Segigeck, the port of the city of Teos, towards the north, was anciently called Geræ. It was peopled with Chalcidensians, who had arrived under Geres. In the wall of the fortification, next the sea, are several inscribed marbles, of a greyish hue, which have been transported from Teos.

Teos is on the slope against Segigeck, and fronting the opposite sea. It is now called Bodrum, but uninhabited, and the port filled with sand; so that the vessels and small craft, employed in carrying on the slight commerce of these places, frequent Geræsticus alone.

And here the classical reader will perhaps recollect that a Roman admiral with a powerful fleet was once in imminent danger of being surprised by the enemy in this port. The relation given by the historian Livy is too minutely connected with the subject not to be inserted.

In the war between Antiochus and the Romans, L. Æmilius Regulus the Prætor, who commanded with eighty ships in these seas, suddenly steered for Teos, on intelligence the city had supplied the royal fleet with provisions; and moreover promised to furnish, for its use, five thousand vessels of wine. He ranged his ships in this port,‡ behind the town, and disembarked his troops with orders to lay waste the territory about the city.

The Teians beholding the ravages thus begun, sent forth orators with the sacred fillets and veils, as suppliants, to the Prætor, but he refused to recal the party, unless the citizens would afford to the Romans the same aid, they had so readily bestowed on the enemy. The orators returned, and the magistrates assembled the people to consult.

In the mean time, Polyxenidas, admiral of the royal fleet, had sailed from Colophon with eighty-nine ships, and being informed of these motions of the Prætor, and that he occupied this port conceived great hopes of attacking the Roman fleet now, in the same manner he lately did the Rhodian at Samos, where he beset the mouth of the port Panormus, in which it lay; this resembling that spot, the promontories approaching each other, and forming an entrance so narrow that two ships could scarcely pass through together. His design was to seize on this strait by night, and secure it with ten ships, to attack the adversary on either side in coming out, and by setting an armed force ashore from the remaining fleet, to overpower him at once by sea and land.

This plan, the historian remarks, would have succeeded; but the Teians complying with his demand, the Prætor put round into the port before the city, which was deemed more commodious for shipping the stores. Eudamus too, who commanded the squadron from Rhodes, was said to have pointed out the peril of their station; two ships entangling and breaking their oars in the strait. The Prætor had also a farther reason for bringing his fleet round, being anxious from the continent, as Antiochus had a camp in the neighbourhood. On gaining the port, both soldiers and sailors, quitting their vessels, were busied in dividing the wine and provisions, when a peasant informed the Prætor that Polyxenidas approached.* The signal was instantly sounded for reimbarking immediately. Tumult and confusion followed, each ship hastening out of port, as soon as manned. The whole fleet proceeded in order of battle to meet the enemy; and a general engagement ensued, in which the Romans proved victorious.

But to return. The favourite deity of the Teians was Dionysius or Bacchus. To him they consecrated their city and territory; and, before the preceding transactions, had solicited the Roman and other states to distinguish both, by decreeing them sacred and an asylum. Several of the answers then given still remain fairly cut on pieces of grey marble, but dispersed; some of the fragments being found in the bagnio at Sygageek, some inserted in the wall, and one over a fountain without the south gate; some also in the burying-grounds round about Sevrihissar. All these are published by Chishull, from copies taken by Consul Sherard in 1709, and again examined in 1716. And the learned editor has prefixed to these literary monuments of the Teians, a delineation of their important idol; to which the reader, curious in that article, is referred.

The spot being therefore the peculiar possession of Dionysius, the Dionysiac artificers, who were very numerous in Asia,‡ and so called from their patron, the reputed inventor of theatrical representation, when incorporated by command of the Kings of Pergamus§ seated here, in the city of their tutelary God; supplying from it Ionia, and the country beyond as far as the

---

* Liv. C. 29.
† The Bacchæ Decree was made Ann. U. C. 559. Ante Ch. 193. Chishull, *Antiquit. Asiatic.*
‡ Καὶ τὸ Διονυσου τοῦ Ἀσίαν ἔθνος καθαρώτατον μέρος τοῦ Ιδιωτικοῦ-Strab. p. 471.
§ Chishull, p. 107, 128.

Hellespont, with the scenic apparatus by contract; until a sedition arising, they fled. This society¹ is marked as prone to tumult, and without faith.

From all these circumstances it might reasonably be presumed, that the Teians did not fail to provide a temple worthy to receive so illustrious an inhabitant as this profitable God, and that his shrine was most richly adorned. The first indeed is sufficiently evinced by the present, though inconsiderable remain, consisting of a confused heap of prostrate marble, now too continually diminishing; the Turks taking from it the grave-stones which it is their custom to place at the head and feet of their deceased; several pieces lying, when we examined it, chipped out, and ready to be so applied. The whole mass is enveloped by bushes and fig-trees.

It is plain from the many furnaces, of which vestiges are seen in and about the heap, that a great consumption of the materials has been formerly made by calcination. In these the ornamental and other members of the fabric have been melted down indiscriminately and without regret. But one broken pedestal has escaped, with an inscription signifying it supported the statue of Claudia Tryphæna, High Priestess of the Goddess Asia, and Priestess of the city God Dionysius; an authentic, though mutilated record of its ancient decoration.

```
ΗΒΟΥΛΗΚΑΙ
ΕΥΣΗΜΕ
ΚΑΤΡΥΦΑΙΝΑΝ
ΑΣΙΑΣΚΑΙΙΕΡΕΑ
ΠΟΛΕΩΣΘΕΟΥ ΔΙ
ΘΥΓΑΤΕΡΑΦΗΣΕΙΟ
ΣΤΡΑΤΟΝΕΙΚΗΣΑΡ
ΑΣΙΑΣΑΝΑΣΤΗΣΑ
ΑΝΔΡΙΑΝΤΑΚΑΛ
ΠΕΙΣΩΜΕΝΗΤΤΟΝΤ
```

At what period the temple was erected cannot perhaps be exactly ascertained, but it probably rose nearly about the same æra with the two following; for as all the temples in this tract were destroyed by Xerxes, except at Ephesus,* it is likely in that age of devotion, the respective cities did not neglect to rebuild, as speedily as possible, such at least as belonged to their tutelary deities; and that all were finished with eager dispatch, but sooner one than another, in proportion to the greatness of the work, and the opulence of its proprietors.

The architect was Hermogenes, who, with Tarchesius and Pythius, asserted the Doric order was improper for sacred edifices. The objections to it are stated by Vitruvius, who remarks that Hermogenes was so convinced, he changed his plan after the marble was ready; and with the materials prepared for constructing a Doric pile, erected this Ionic temple.†

He is recorded also as the author of a treatise on the Ionic temple of Diana at Magnesia, which was pseudo-dipteral; and of one on this, which was hexastyle, and is cited by Vitruvius as an example of the eustyle.‡ Rome not affording one. He adds, it was Hermogenes, who scaled the proportions he delivers, and who first invented the octastyle pseudo-dipteral, taking away the interior range of columns from the dipteral, and thus diminishing both the labour and expense; giving ample room for walking round the cell without debasing the aspect; preserving in his distribution, the dignity of the entire work without its superfluities; the pteroma, and disposition of columns about the cell, having been contrived that the aspect might have majesty from the narrowness of the intercolumniations. And, moreover, the space thus acquired was convenient for the accommodation of the multitude, if occasionally surprised and detained by sudden and violent showers. Vitruvius infers that Hermogenes had effected this in his works with great sagacity and skill, leaving to posterity sources, from which it might deduce the reasons of his improvements.

From such an eulogium on its architect, this temple may justly arrogate an additional importance; being respectable, as the sole, though imperfect monument of so eminent a master; and useful both as an evidence and illustration of his doctrines.

---

* Ἔφη τῶν τε ναῶν τῶν Ἀσίηνῶν Ἀπόλλωνος τε τοῦ Βραγχίδεω κατέπρησε ὁ τῶν Περςέων στρατὸς κατὰ τὰ αὐτὰ τοῖσι ἐνθαῦτα τε Ἴωσι. *Strabo,* p. 633.

† Nonnulli antiqui Architecti negaverunt Dorico genere ædes sacras oportere fieri, quod mendosæ et incommodæ in his symmetriæ conficiebantur.—Itaque negavit Tarchesius, item Pythius, non minus Hermogenes. Nam is, cum paratam habuisset marmoris copiam in Dorici ædis perfectionem, commutavit, et ex eadem copia eam Ionicam Libero patri fecit. *Vitruv.* L. iv. c. 3.

‡ Hujus exemplar Romæ nullum habemus, sed in Asia Teo hexastylon Liberi patris. Eas autem symmetrias consituit Hermogenes, qui etiam primus octastylou pseudodipteri rationem invenit. Ex dipteri enim ædis symmetria sustulit interiores ordines columnarum xxxviii, eaque ratione sumptus operasque compendii fecit. Is in medio ambulationi laxamentum egregie circa cellam fecit, de aspectuque nihil imminuit, sed sine desiderio supervacuorum conservavit auctoritatem totius operis distributione. Pteromatos enim ratio et columnarum circum ædem dispositio ideo est inventa, ut aspectus propter asperitatem intercolumniorum haberet auctoritatem. Præterea si ex imbrium aqua vis occupaverit et intercluserit hominum multitudinem, ut habeat in æde circaque cellam cum laxamento liberam moram. Hæc autem ita explicantur in Pseudodipteris ædium dispositionibus: quare videtur acuta magnaque sollertia effectus operum Hermogenis fecisse, reliquisseque fontes unde posteri possent haurire disciplinarum rationes. *Vitruv.* L. iii. MSS.

PLATE I.

VIEW OF THE TEMPLE OF BACCHUS AT TEOS.

PLATE II.

ORDER OF THE COLUMNS.

Circumstances having arisen to prevent the mission of the Society of Dilettanti from visiting Teos, nothing additional is offered to the reader on the subject of the Temple of Bacchus there. This is the less to be regretted, since the discoveries in other parts of Asia Minor have enabled the Society to exhibit in the present volume a specimen of three varieties of Ionic temples, hexastyle, octastyle, and decastyle.

In the first edition of this Work an engraving was given of the supposed front of the temple restored, as to the general proportions, from the description given by Vitruvius of eustyle temples; of which kind he instances the temple at Teos as an example. With respect to the passage of this author, in which allusion is made to the Teian temple, it must be observed in the first place, that all the manuscripts describe the temple to have been hexastyle, or with six columns in front, and, consequently, with a single peristyle. The opinion hitherto entertained, that the temple in question was of a more magnificent description of buildings, has arisen from a supposed obscurity in the text of Vitruvius. To obviate an apparent difficulty the commentators have been obliged to alter two words, and substitute, in the first place, *octastylos* for *hexastylos*, and in the second to read *dipteros* for *monopteros*. The necessity for either correction does not exist: for it is evident, that Vitruvius merely makes use of the word monopteros, in contradistinction to dipteros, in the same passage. But if it should be contended, that the word is used in the restricted sense which the beginning of the eighth chapter, in the fourth book, seems to imply, it will be safer to hazard one correction than two; and by reading *peripteros* for *monopteros* words of similar import, there can be no ground whatever for farther correction, and the temple of Bacchus at Teos must be regarded as an example of a more simple kind of building. On this account, therefore, the elevation of the temple, given in the first edition, is omitted in the present; the object of which is to correct the errors which, either through the ignorance prevailing on the subject of Grecian architecture, or the inadequacy of the means employed to obtain access to the substructure of the ruins, unavoidably found their way into the first representations of the architecture of the Grecian colonies. There is, however, another reason why, all other motives set aside, the suppression of the plate was considered imperiously necessary. Vitruvius, in his Treatise on architecture, attempted to reduce the architecture of Greece to certain invariable rules, by which, as he imagined, the architects of old were guided in the construction of their temples. According to the principle which he conjectured he had discovered, the intervals between the columns of temples bear a certain ratio to the lower diameter of the columns; and accordingly as this proportion was one and a half, two, or three to one, the temples were classed as Pycnostyle, Systyle, or Diastyle. In the temples of Greece, however, we find no such invariable rules, although instances are known, where these precise proportions actually occur; we have temples with perhaps all the intermediate proportions, from one and a quarter to three diameters; some of these would therefore fall without his assumed arrangement, and a new hypothesis become necessary. Thus, for instance, where the intervals were more than one and a half and less than two, or more than two and less than three, another principle must be sought; unless, by enlarging the central interval, the others could be reduced to these limits and the whole extent of the front thus made to correspond with the proportions assigned in the writings of the Greek architects. This conjectural disposition of the columns received apparent support from the practice which, in a limited degree, obtained amongst the architects of Greece in their Doric edifices. We have examples of a wider centre interval in the several propylæa of Athens, Eleusis, and Sunium; and the almost constant observance of a similar practice in the temples of Egypt. In buildings, however, of the Ionic order, the enlargement of a central opening, as a measure of necessity or convenience, was in no degree essential, because of the greater disparity between the diameters of the columns and the intervals. And it is to be observed that this enlargement in the Doric order was only permitted in propylæa or gateways, through which there was a constant traffic, or in the stoas or porticoes, where, the columns being of small dimensions, a rigid adherence to principle would have rendered the intervals of inconvenient contraction.

Had the Ionic order prevailed in the propylæa of Athens and Eleusis the intervals, supposing the columns to have been of equal magnitude, would have been ten feet; an ample width for the passage of carriages. For this reason it is, that even in the propylæa of the Ionic order, the central intervals, as we shall see hereafter, were not always enlarged, although in a future work we shall produce examples of a wider interval in similar buildings, where the columns being small, the intervals would have been inconveniently so, without departing from the greater severity observed in sacred edifices.

From all that has hitherto reached us relating to the architecture of the Greeks, we come to this conclusion—that the enlargement of the central intervals is a departure from rule, more rare in the Ionic order than in the Doric; and that no ancient example, of the many known to us, affords authority for such a relaxation in temples of either order.

Such exceptions, however, afforded to Vitruvius the ground-work for the species of temple which he calls eustyle; why the temple of Bacchus at Teos should be mentioned by him in illustration of his theory, we have already offered a conjecture.

TEOS.

Relying upon the authority of Vitruvius, the editors of the first edition of this work being possessed of some details of the Temple at Teos, attempted a representation of the eastern front, which is given in the plate, the suppression of which we have now attempted to justify to the readers of the present publication.

PLATE II.

Fig. 1. The Base of the Columns, with the lower part of the Shaft.

The plinth, lower torus, and scotia, with its fillets, are of one piece of marble. The upper torus, with an astragal, is annexed to the apophyges of the column, probably to strengthen and preserve it from accident and injury, the projecture being very great.

The small diminution of this column proves that the two portions of the shaft belonged to different columns; the upper part, probably to one of the external range; and the lower to the front either of the pronaos or posticum, in both which the columns were less in diameter than in the external range, as is evident from the Temple of Jupiter Olympius at Athens, and various other examples. And from this circumstance, the reason of that great projecture of the apophyges noted above is plain; for, if the bases of the external and internal columns of the dipteros were of the same proportions, the apophyges both of the one and the other must likewise be of the same; and, consequently, the smaller the diameter is, of the internal columns, the greater will be the projecture of the apophyges. But a different symmetry is observed in the bases of the Temple of Jupiter Olympius; for the external bases have plinths, and are in height the semi-diameter of their columns: but the internal have none, and are placed upon a step, which raised the pavement within the internal range of the dipteros, its whole height above that within the external; on which account the internal columns are less in altitude than the external by the height of the step, as well as less in diameter. The mouldings also of the internal bases are much higher than those of the external; nor have they any connexion with each other, except in the diameter of their lower torus; but the mouldings of the internal, being higher, have a greater projecture, which (as the diameter of the lower torus is the same in both) contracts the upper torus, and makes it less than in the external bases. Thus the architect diminished the great projecture of the apophyges remarked in this column.

Fig. 2. The capital and architrave, with the upper part of the shaft of the columns.

The capital, astragal, and apotheosis, with a small part of the shaft, are of one piece of marble.

The proportions of this capital, and the analogy it has to the base, and lower part of the column, may be collected from hence: if the upper part of the shaft be divided into twenty-one parts, the diameter of the column below will be (as it was found by the actual measurement) twenty-two, and the astragal under the capital twenty-two and a half; the length and breadth of the abacus of the capital twenty-four, and the diameter of the echinus twenty-seven, which is equal to the diameter of the astragal under the apophyges of the column: the height of the capital will be nine parts, and including the volutes, thirteen and a half, which is the semi-diameter of the echinus: this also is the height of the base, including the plinth; and without that, one third of the length of the abacus of the capital. All these proportions correspond as nearly with the measures as can be expected, especially considering the latter as collected from several different fragments.

The thickness of the architrave could not be obtained; so that, in placing it upon the capital, with the front perpendicular over the border in the face of the volutes, the example of the temple on the Ilissus at Athens has been followed; the breadth of the soffit of the architrave being found in the Greek buildings always to exceed the diameter of the neck of the column, not only in this order, but also in the Doric and Corinthian.

Fig. 3. A section through the front of the capital and architrave.

The latter has a compartment in the soffit, ornamented with a defaced scroll surrounded with a bead.

Fig. 4. A section through the profile of the capital.

The pulvini or pillows of the volutes were decorated with leaves, but so much defaced, the species was not distinguishable; for which reason the plan of the capital, and the elevation of the profile are omitted.

Fig. 5. The contour of the volute.

Palladio's method of describing the volute agrees in general extremely well with these measures, except in the breadth, which was very difficult to take.

PLATE III

Fig. 1. The cornice of the temple. The fragment of a lion's head, and a piece of ornament, are the only remains that could be discovered.

Fig. 2. An architrave and frize, of one piece of marble, decorated with a patera and festoons of laurel, in a Turkish burying-ground by a mosque at Segigeek.

It is observable, that the ovolo in the cymatium of the architrave is wrought flat, with a little fillet in the upper part of it.

Fig. 3. A section through the soffit of the architrave, which has a compartment surrounded with an ovolo wrought also flat. The mouldings of this fragment are also executed with great accuracy and neatness.

Fig. 4. A pedestal, and square base, of one piece of white marble, near the south gate at Segigeek. The mouldings of the base project over the die of the pedestal.

These marbles have a place here, as it is not doubted but they belonged formerly to Teos.

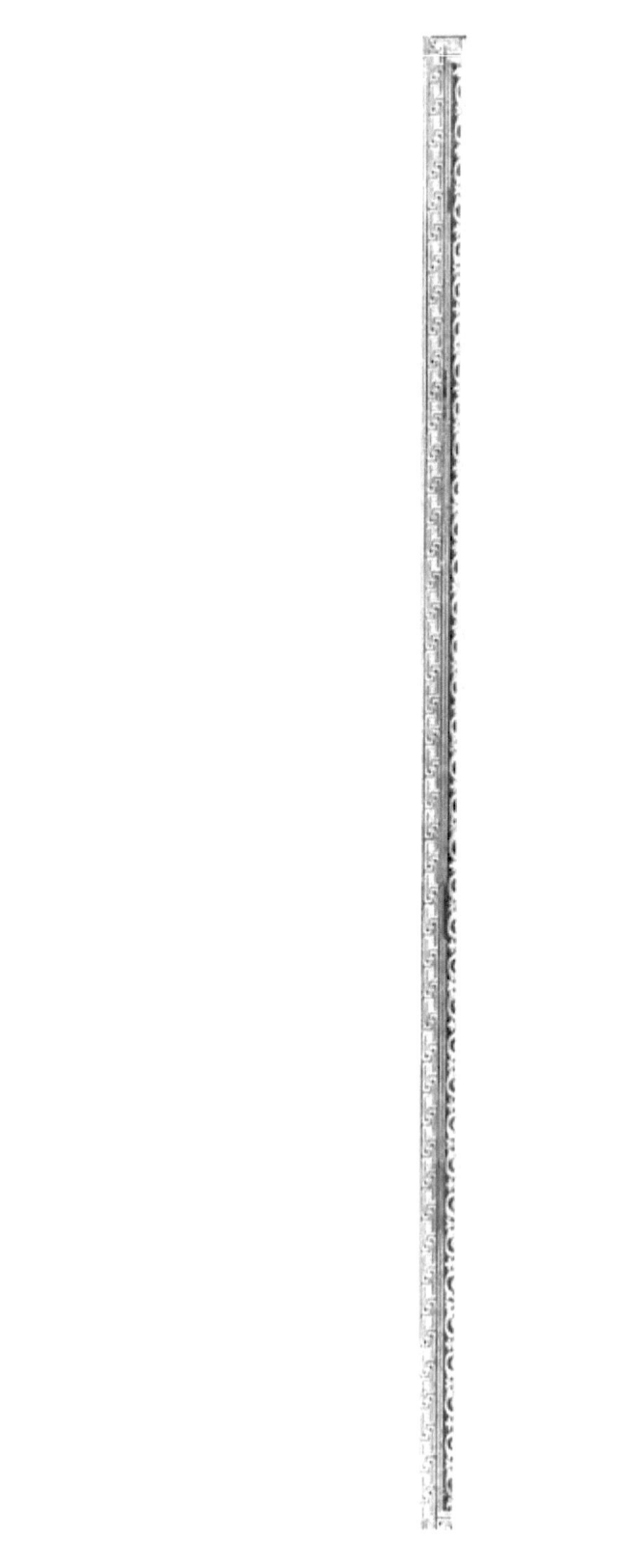

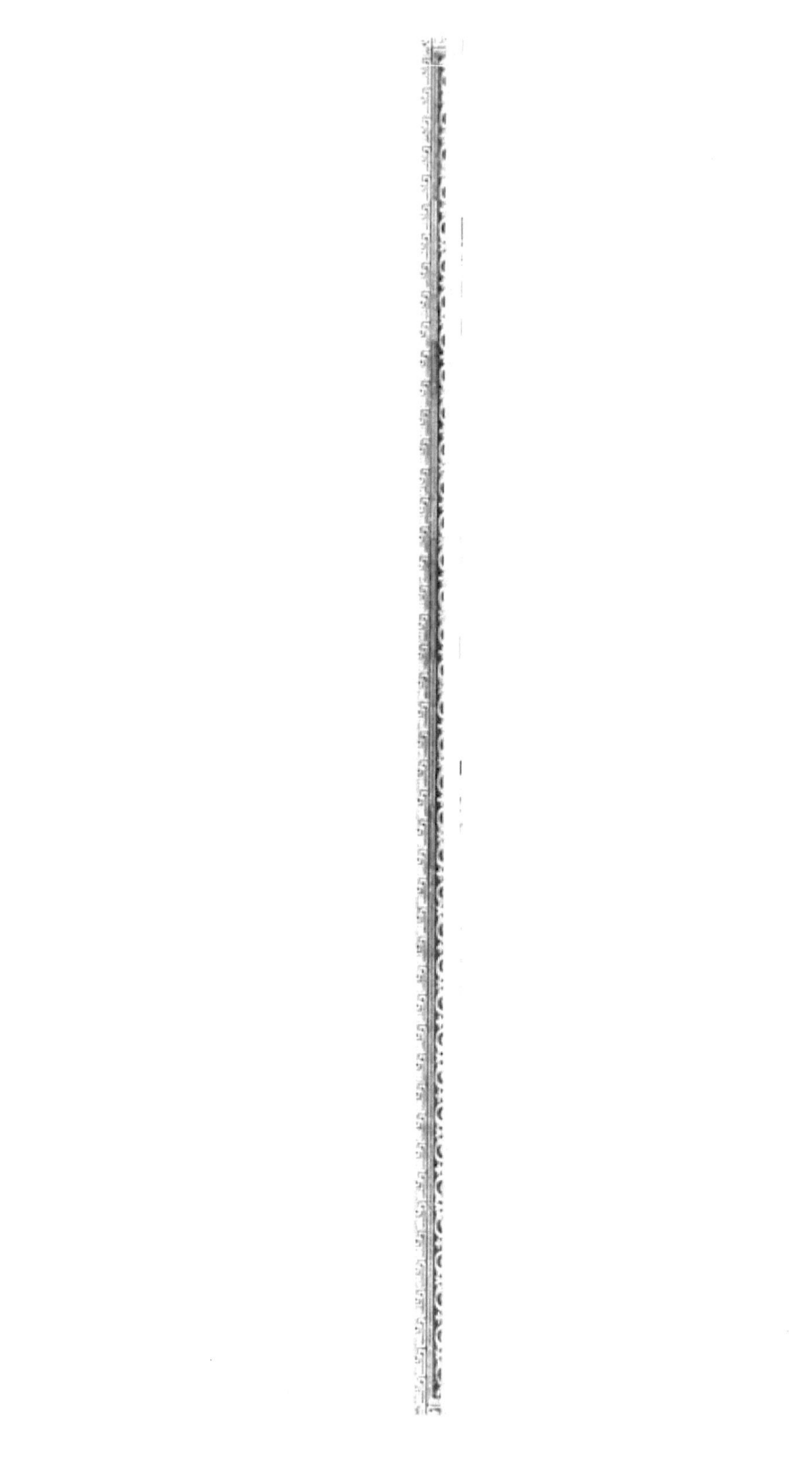

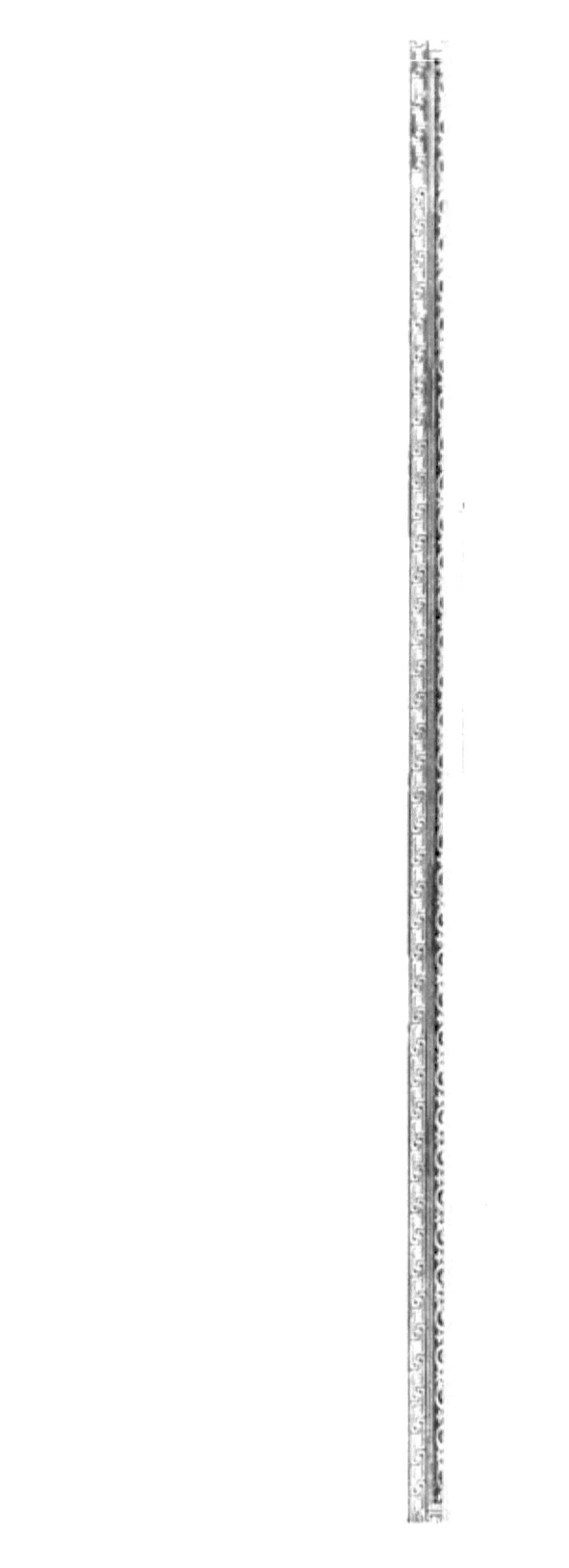

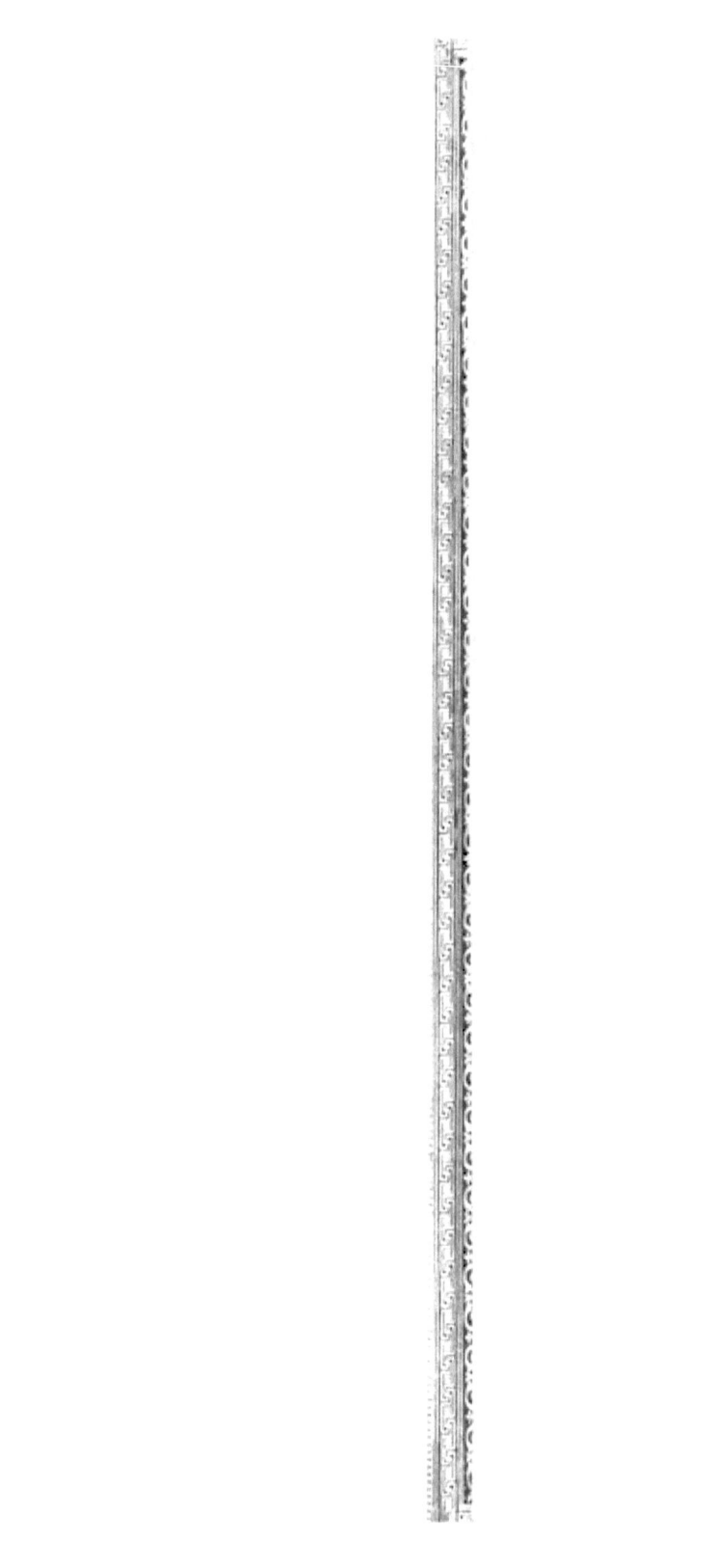

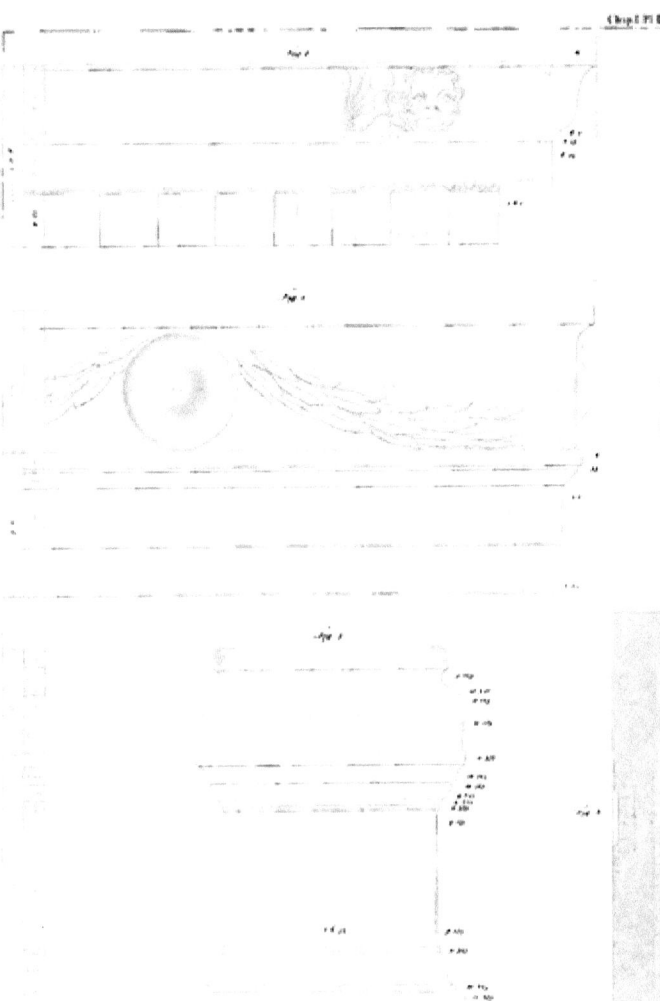

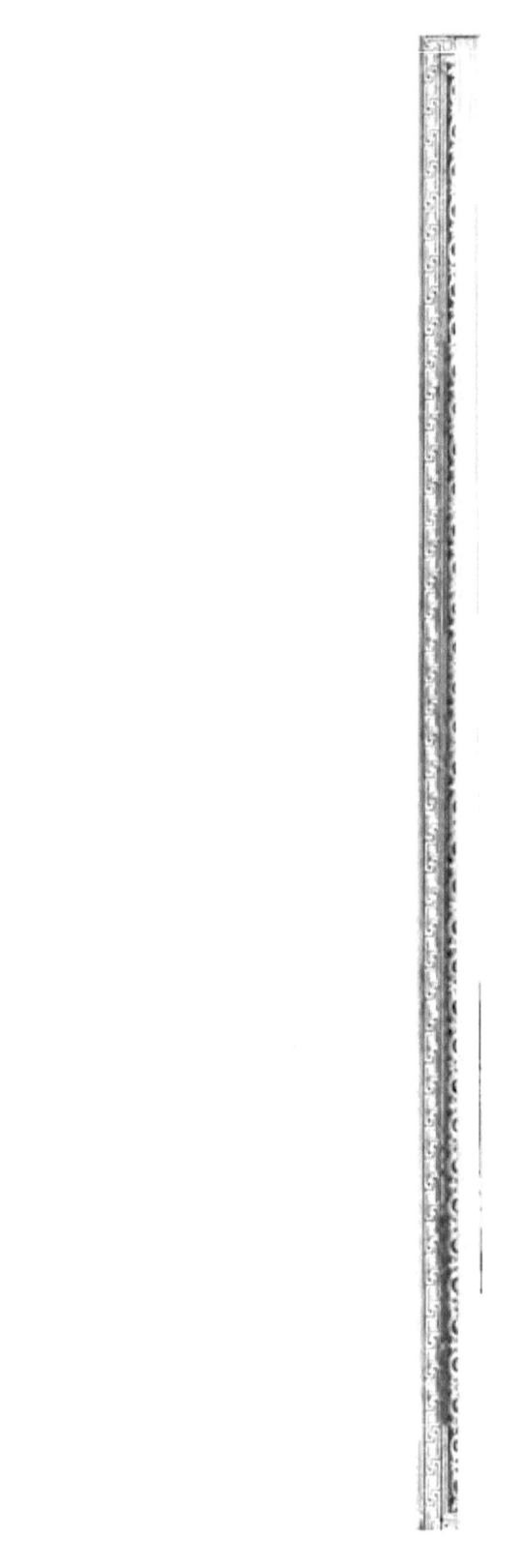

CHAPTER II.

PRIENE.

PRIENE was situated on the south side of a mountain called Mycale. It now commands an extensive view over a fine plain intersected by a winding water-course approaching near to the walls, and by the river Maeander.

The alteration in the topography of this tract, gradually produced in a long series of time, will be alluded to in the description of the plain of the Maeander. At present, therefore, we shall remark only in general, that Priene, though now seen as an inland city, was once on the sea, and had two ports; the plain between it and Miletus was a large bay; and the Maeander, which now prolongs its course much beyond, once glided smoothly* into it.

These changes are so great as to bewilder and perplex the traveller, unless he is in possession of a clue, and may be assigned as the probable reason why so remarkable a portion of ancient Ionia is at present so little visited or known; the only tour through this tract, as yet given to the public, being that which was undertaken in 1673, by certain English merchants from Smyrna.† It would be ungenerous to censure this journey as superficial and unsatisfactory, while it merits so much applause for the liberal design and communicative spirit of the party, which thus opened as it were a way, although hitherto almost unfrequented, for the benefit of future inquirers.

* Lorem ipsum auct. Plin. L. v. c. 29.   † Published by Wheler in 1682, as also by Spon.

Priene fell by accident into their route, and is mentioned as a village called Samsun, the name, by which and Samsun-calesi it is still known. The antiquities noted by them are ruins in general, a pillar, and a defaced inscription.* It is now a large and populous village.

The whole space within the walls, of which almost the entire circuit remains standing, and in some parts several feet high, is strewed over with rubbish or scattered fragments of marble edifices. The ruined churches are monuments of the piety of its more modern inhabitants; as the vestiges of a theatre, of a stadium, and more particularly the splendid heap formed by the ruins of the temple, are of the taste and magnificence of its more flourishing possessors. The acropolis was on a flat above the precipice.

The view will furnish a much clearer idea of the situation and present state of the temple, than it is in the power of words to convey. The capitals exquisitely worked, and the rich fragments of ancient sculpture, afford equal matter of admiration and regret; nor can the trunks of the maimed statues, or a long but defaced inscription, be viewed, without a wish to know what illustrious persons those represented, and what meritorious citizen, public treaty, or private compact, this recorded.

In the article of Teos it is remarked, that Xerxes destroyed all the temples in Ionia except at Ephesus. How soon the Prieneans after that fatal era began to rebuild this, and what progress they had made, before Alexander's time, or whether it still lied in ruins when he entered upon his expedition, is uncertain. But this mighty conqueror, who regarded Asia as his patrimony,† and with this idea had prohibited the pillage on his first landing, was as studious to adorn, as the flying Persian had been ready to deface it; not only founding new cities, but restoring the pristine splendor of the old, and re-erecting the temples which the other had thrown down, extending his pious care even to the devastation made at Babylon.‡ Priene also shared his favour, as is evinced by the following valuable record, happily preserved to us by a stone, which belonged to one of the antæ, now lying at the east end of the heap, in large characters most beautifully formed and cut

ΒΑΣΙΛΕΥΣΑΛΕΞΑΝΔΡΟΣ
ΑΝΕΘΗΚΕΤΟΝΝΑΟΝ
ΑΘΗΝΑΙΗΙΠΟΛΙΑΔΙ

KING ALEXANDER
DEDICATED THE TEMPLE
TO MINERVA CIVICA.

---

* Wheler, p. 264.

† Ptolemæorum causæ nequis, quod ut Macedoniæ, Epirique habebant, tamdiu dividi, sibi Asiam velleent prædium [...] Asia prædium prævestorum rebelles præditur, nec præde solus ea, quæ parvorum veteres. Justin. c. 6.

‡ Ὁ γαρ τε Δαρειου τε μετρα ες τροπον τα Βαβυλωνος, μητρῳος τε μητροπολις—ταδε τοι πως, ουτος και τα αλλα ὁσα τα βαρβαρων ὑβρις καθαιραφαι, ινα τι τε Ελλαδι ουσαν προσεθηκεν. Αλεξανδρος δε ως τα ιερον ανωρθωσε.—ἐτει δε ανωλιαδης μεγαλαφωνος ανδραπα τι τροπω, ης παιδα εινδραπιαν εις τυξαλης τοις τροπους τε ὑρχω ιρμοσαπιοσαν. Arrian. l. vii. p. 286. Ed. Gron.

This stone, which is inscribed also on one side, with the many other fragments by it, seems to indicate, that the fronts and external faces of the antæ were covered with inscriptions; and from the degrees of magnitude in the letter, it may be conjectured, a regard was had to perspective, the greater being higher, and more remote, the smaller nearer to the eye; so that, at the proper point of view for reading, all might appear nearly of the same proportion. Many of these stones were much too ponderous to be turned up, or moved aside, by any strength or power we could apply; which is the more to be regretted, as the legends of several are perfectly uninjured. We carefully copied those portions to which we could gain access; but these, as not relating to the history of the temple, are reserved for publication in our collection of inscriptions.

The above memorial may perhaps be deemed decisive in respect to the age of the fabric: but it should be remembered, that Alexander was ambitious of inscribing such works; and it will be unfair to conclude that this was not begun, if not far advanced or nearly finished, when he entered Asia; since on his arrival at Ephesus in his way hither, it is related, that finding the Temple of Diana, which had been destroyed by Herostratus about the time of his birth, rebuilding under the direction of Dinocrates, he offered the Ephesians to defray all their past expenses, and to complete the edifice, for the gratification, which, it appears, he procured at Priene, to wit, the privilege of inscribing it as the dedicator; and this, trifling as it may seem, was then esteemed so honourable and important, that he could not obtain it even on terms so very liberal and magnificent.

The architect of this august temple was the Pythæus, or, as he is named in another passage, Philoss, mentioned in the article of Teos. The ruin, as Vitruvius also does, may bear testimony to the nobleness of his genius. He described it in a written exposition; and it is recorded, he conceived so highly of his profession, as to assert in his commentaries, that it behoved an architect to excel more in all arts and sciences, even than the individuals who had carried each by their application and industry, to the summit of reputation.

But, glorious as this fabric was when entire, it presented also another object of admiration to the heathen traveller; for Pausanias, after affirming that Ionia was adorned with temples, such as no other province could boast, and enumerating the principal, adds, " You would be delighted too with that of Minerva at Priene, on account of the statue."

PLATE I.

MAP OF THE COURSE OF THE MÆANDER.

Wheler* and Spon are indebted for the account which they have published of this region to a journey begun in June, 1673, by Dr Pickering and some merchants of Smyrna. These travellers, quitting Changlee about four in the morning, gained the top of Mycale, on which they had an extensive view, and one of them designed the mazes of the Mæander. They descended by a difficult and narrow track, and in two hours came into the plain, having left behind the remains of a castle eastward. From Samsun, or Priene, then a village at the foot of Mycale, they passed through a large plain to the Mæander, called by the Turks Boiuc-Mänder, or the *Great Mæander*, which they crossed at a ferry, where it was about sixteen fathom broad, and as many deep in the middle, as the guide informed them, with the current very swift. About two hours after this, they arrived at Palasha, where they pitched their tents on the banks of a large river, which, running through a great lake, falls into the Mæander.

The reader will observe that these travellers crossed the river but once between Samsun and Palasha. The ferry therefore was below the junction of the two beds. There the stream was called *the Great Mæander*, probably to distinguish it, not, as has been supposed, from the Cayster, which is remote from the other, or *Little River*, which it receives. This they mistook for the principal stream, being ignorant of the true Mæander, with which the lake of Myûs communicates, and which runs by Palasha. This also lies beneath them, when on mount Mycale, and was seen distinctly as in a chart. Their draughtsmen delineated its turnings and windings for those of the old and famous river; and its mazes, which helped to impose on them, prevented even the suspicion of an error.

The Mæander, among the rivers of Asia Minor, was anciently noted for the production of new land. The stream, it was remarked, in passing through the ploughed grounds of Phrygia and Caria, collected much slime, and bringing it down continually, added to the coast at its mouth.

The Mæander was indictable for removing the soil when its margin tumbled in; and the person, who recovered damages, was paid from the income of the ferries. The downfals were very frequent, and are supposed, with probability, to be the cause of the curvature of the bed; the earth carried away from one part lodging in another, and replacing the loss sustained on one side by adding to the opposite bank.

* Page 267.

PRIENE.

The stream crosses from near mount Messogis to the foot of Titanus, opposite to Priene; and on that side it continues, running toward the mouth of the lake of Myûs. Probably the level of the intermediate plain determined it in that course; the soil washed from Mycale, or supplied by the torrent, raising the surface there, and forbidding its approach. The current, repelled by the rocks of Chebasha, and contracted about the ferry, wore its present channel, while the mud was soft and yielding; and the bed, which we passed near them, was created from the same obstruction, the water after floods running off there more forcibly, as meeting with more resistance.

The river turns from the mouth of the lake, with many windings, through groves of tamarisk, toward Miletus; proceeding by the right wing of the theatre in mazes to the sea, which is in view, and distant, as we computed about eight miles; the plain smooth and level as a bowling-green, except certain knolls extant in it, near mid-way before Miletus. One of these, the northernmost, is seen distinct, as a hillock; and on a larger is a village named Petaiotis. In that part is the union of the watercourse of Priene with the river, which winds south of the hillock, and lies on its margin, two or more miles beyond a small fortress. The extremity of the plain by the shore appeared, from the precipice of Priene, marshy, or bare, and like mud. Such was the face of this region when we saw it. How different from its aspect, when the mountains were boundaries of a gulf, and Miletus, Myûs, and Priene, maritime cities!

Strabo, a geographer as exact as comprehensive, whose volume is indeed an inestimable treasure, will furnish us, as it were, with a chart, enabling us to contemplate this coast, as it existed toward the commencement of the Christian æra; before a famous sophist affirmed of it, that the river had taken the sea from the navigator, and given it to the husbandman to be divided into fields; that furrows were seen in the place of waves, and kids sporting in the room of dolphins; and that instead of hearing the hoarse mariner, you were delighted with the sweet echo of the pastoral pipe.

Miletus had then four ports, one of them very capacious; and before it was a cluster of small islands. Beyond Miletus, the coast winding, was a bay called the Latmian, from Latmus, the adjacent mountain. In this bay was "Heraclea under Latmus," a small town, once called Latmus, with a road for vessels; and near that place, after crossing a rivulet, was a cavern or grotto, with the sepulchre of Endymion. On this mountain, it was fabled, Luna cast that hero and hunter into a profound sleep, to have the pleasure of saluting him. After Heraclea was Pyrrha, an inconsiderable town, the distance between them by sea about one hundred stadia, or twelve miles and a half. From Miletus to Heraclea was a little more, coasting the bay; but from Miletus to Pyrrha,*

---

* The Latin interpreter of Strabo has omitted the words *From Miletus to Pyrrha.* See also Cellarius, p. 52.

The geographer, after mentioning slightly Pyrrha and Heraclea as inconsiderable towns, advertises his reader, that the compass of his work requires him not to dwell but on places of note. This passage is grossly misstated. The interpreter will frequently mislead those who attend not to the original; and is, in this instance, the sole cause why Wheler, finding himself puzzled, suspects Strabo to be less accurate in this portion of his work, than he pretends to be.

The river running by the theatre of Miletus perplexed Wheler exceedingly. He supposes Miletus to have been Pyrrha, and Branchidæ to be Heraclea. Spon, with the same materials, supposes the mention of any difficulty;

in a straight course, was only thirty stadia, or three miles and three quarters, so much longer was the voyage by the shore. From Pyrrha to the mouth of the Mæander were fifty stadia, or six miles and a quarter, the ground slimy and marshy. From hence there was a navigation to Myûs* in skiffs, or small vessels, a distance of thirty stadia. After the mouth of the Mæander was the coast against Priene. The sea had once washed the wall of this city, and it had two ports, one of which shut up; but then it was seen within land, forty stadia, or five miles, above the shore.

The principal island in the cluster before Miletus was Lade. There, when invaded by Darius, the Ionians assembled three hundred and sixty triremes, and engaged his fleet of six hundred. The Milesians had eighty ships, and formed the wing toward the east. Next to them were the Prieneans with twelve, and the Myusians with three. The island was afterwards seized by Alexander; and, while he besieged Miletus, was the station of the Greek admiral, who blocked up the port. The Milesians, when he was about to storm the city, tried to escape, some in skiffs, some swimming on their bucklers, but were intercepted; only three hundred getting to a steep islet, which they resolved to defend. This probably was one by Lade. Two, near Miletus, called Camelida, *the Camels*, were among the less considerable. A single one, it is likely the northernmost hillock, was called Asteria, from Asterius, whose skeleton, remarkable for its size, was shown there. He reigned, it is related, before the Ionic migration. By the Tragiæ, probably mud-banks and shoals formed by the river, were other islets, the stations of robbers.

"Nature," says Pliny, "has taken islands from the sea, and joined them to the continent; from Miletus, Dromiscos and Perne; and Hybanda, once an island of Ionia, is now two hundred stadia, twenty-five miles, from the coast." Nature in this district was the Mæander, and the islands here specified are perhaps the rocks of Oselashà. The river has been, as it were, the parent of its own bed.

The bay, on which Myûs was once seated, became a lake, when the Mæander, by lodging slime at the mouth, had cut off the ingress of the salt-water. The mountains were an obstacle, or the whole recess would have been filled, and converted into a plain. Their rills also supplied the fresh water, which generated the gnats. The land grew, as it were, daily, and was continually removing the sea farther from the lake. The mouth of the Mæander was then seen between

---

and, on the authority of the inscription on the theatre, boldly calls the place Miletus. Cellarius prefers the opinion of Wheler. He cites Strabo to prove the distance between Miletus and the mouth of the river was CX. stadia; and observing it only X. in Pliny, supposes the numeral C omitted. But the calculation from Strabo is imperfect and erroneous, the emendation of Pliny neither well founded nor necessary; and it happens, that Spon is superficially right, while Cellarius with Wheler is learnedly mistaken.

It were easy to enlarge on the errors of Cellarius in this part of his work, and to reflect back the unmerited censures which he bestows on the ancient writers, who have treated on the places.

We may with reason wonder, that no scholars close to these intricacies and seeming contradictions, so that we have given, has hitherto escaped the modern travellers, geographers, and annotators, in general; especially as each class professes to take Strabo for their surest guide, or principal counsel.

* The distance between Miletus and Myûs, by water, seems to have been one hundred and ten stadia, or thirteen and three quarters:

From Miletus to Pyrrha	30
From Pyrrha to the mouth of the Mæander	50
From thence to Myûs	30

Miletus and Priene; and this city had a wide plain before it. Afterwards it approached within ten stadia, or a mile and a quarter, of Miletus; and the bays above that city were rendered firm ground. The traveller, who shall ride along the foot of mount Latmus, eastward from Miletus, will, I doubt not, discover the site of Heracleia; and the rivulet may direct him even now to the cave of Endymion. Pyrrha has been mentioned as within land. The space between Priene and Miletus was added, in no long time to the continent. The ports of this city ceased to be navigable; and, by degrees, Lade and Asteria, and the islets near them, were encircled with soil. Before this happened, the water-course of Priene entered the sea, separate from the Mæander.

Miletus, deprived by the Mæander of the principal advantages of its situation, experienced, with the cities its neighbours, a gradual decay, which will end in total extinction, as it were, by a natural death, after a lingering illness. The progress of the changes, as might be expected, were unattended to in the barbarous ages, as not sudden, or unnoticed, as not important. But we are informed, that a place by the shore, where the river in the ninth century entered the sea, was called *the Gardens*; and that the Greek emperor Manuel, finding the region well watered and beautiful to the eye, resolved to refresh his army there, and to forget the toils of war in the pleasures of the chase.

From the alterations already effected, we may infer, that the Mæander will still continue to encroach; that the recent earth, now soft, will harden, and the present marshes be dry. The shore will in time protrude so far, that the promontories, which now shelter it, will be seen inland. It will unite with Samos, and in a series of years extend to remoter islands, if the soil, while fresh and yielding, be not carried away by some current setting without the mountains. If this happen, it will be distributed along the coast, or wafted elsewhere in the tide, and form new plains. Some barren rock of the adjacent deep may be enriched with a fertile domain, and other cities rise and flourish from the bounty of the Mæander.

The story of Myûs is remarkable, but not singular. A town by Pergamum had suffered in the same manner. Myûs originally was seated on a bay of the sea, not large, but abounding in fish. Hence, this city was given to Themistocles to furnish that article for his table. The bay changed into a lake, and become fresh. Myriads of gnats swarmed on it, and the town was devoured, as it were, from the water. The Myusians retired from this enemy to Miletus, carrying away all their moveables and the statues of their gods. They were incorporated with the Milesians, and sacrificed, and gave their suffrage with them at the Panionian congress. A writer of the second century relates, that nothing remained at Myûs in his time, but a temple of Bacchus of white stone or marble.

The site of Myûs is as romantic as its fortune was extraordinary. The wall incloses a mass of naked rocks rudely piled, of a dark dismal hue, with precipices and vast hollows, from which perhaps stone has been cut. A few huts, inhabited by Turkish families, are of the same colour, and scarcely distinguishable. Beyond these, fronting the lake, there is a theatre hewn in the mountain, with some mossy remnants of the wall of the proscenium; but the marble seats are removed. Between the huts and the lake are several terraces with steps cut as at Priene. One, a quadrangular area edged with marble fragments, is conjectured to have been the Agora. By another were stones ornamented with shields of a circular form. But the principal and most conspicuous ruin is the small temple of Bacchus, which is seated on an abrupt rock, with the front only, which is toward the east, accessible. The roof is destroyed. The cell is well built, of smooth stone, with a brown crust on it. The portico was in Antis. It has been used as a church, and the entrance walled up with patch-work. The marbles, which lie scattered about, the broken columns, and mutilated statues, all witness a remote antiquity. The city wall was constructed, like that at Ephesus, with square towers, and is still standing, except toward the water. It runs up the mountain-slope so far as to be in some places hardly discernible.

Without the city are the cemeteries of its early inhabitants; graves cut in the rock, of all sizes, suited to the human stature at different ages, with innumerable flat stones, which served as lids. Some are yet covered, and many open, and, by the lake, filled with water. The lids are overgrown with a short, dry, brown moss, their very aspect evincing old age. An inscription, close by a small hut in a narrow pass of the mountain westward, on marble, in large characters, records a son of Seleucus, who died young, and the affliction of his parents; concluding with a tender expostulation with them on the inefficacy and impropriety of their immoderate sorrow. Nearer the city, among some trees, is a well, with the base of a column perforated on the mouth.

It may be inferred from the vestiges of monasteries and churches, which are numerous, that Myûs was repeopled when monachism, spreading from Egypt, towards the end of the fourth century, extended itself over the Greek and Latin empires. The lake abounding in fish, afforded an important article of diet under a ritual, which enjoined frequent abstinence from flesh. It probably contributed to render this place, which appears to have been the grand resort of devotees and anchorites, a nursery of saints, another mount Athos.

At the head of the lake are the remains of several buildings. Here probably stood Thymbria, within four stadia of Myûs. Near it was a charonium, or sacred cavern, one of those supposed by the ancients to communicate with the infernal regions, and to be filled with the deadly vapours of lake Avernus.

The lake is visible from Priene and Miletus. It is greater in length than in width; the water is brackish. There are several rocky islets within its circuit; one near Myûs is surrounded with a wall of common masonry, inclosing the ruins of a church. Amongst the fragments was found a marble with a sepulchral inscription to " Heraclides son of Satacles, Neochorus to Hecate." This temple was probably near the charonium of Thymbria. The Neochori had the general care of the temples to which they belonged, and the office was accounted very honourable. It was sometimes conferred on cities, and is found inscribed among their titles.

The Greek emperor Manuel encamped near this lake with his army, about the year 867. "His camp," says Cinnamus, "was situated towards the mouths of the Meander. There an immense quantity of water issues forth at the foot of the mountains, as it were the produce of a thousand springs; and, spreading a deluge over the adjacent country, first composes a lake, then, forming for itself a deep bed, becomes a river." Its junction with the Meander is computed to be half a mile in length. The city of Myüs had anciently an intercourse by water with Miletus.

PLATE II.

MAP OF PRIENE.

The acropolis is situated upon a natural terrace, incircled, excepting towards the plain, by an ancient wall of the masonry termed pseudisodomum. This has been repaired and made tenable in a later age by additional out-works. A steep, high and naked rock rises behind, and the terrace terminates in front, in a most abrupt and formidable precipice, whence the spectator looks down with awe on the diminutive objects beneath. The massive heap of the temple below appears to the naked eye but as chippings of marble.

A winding track leads down from the acropolis to the city; the steps cut in the rock are narrow; the path no wider than sufficient to permit the approach of a single person.

The temple of Minerva-Polias, although prostrate, is one of the remains of Ionian elegance and grandeur too considerable to be hastily or slightly examined. When entire it overlooked the city, which was seated on the side of the mountain on terraces cut out of the slope, descending in gradation to the edge of the plain. The communication from one terrace to another was by staircases cut in the solid rock, many of which are still remaining. Below the temple are the ruins of the Agora, consisting of fragments of the Doric and Ionic orders of architecture.

On a lower terrace the remains of a stadium are seen, one of its sides being supported by the ancient wall of the city, which is strengthened by buttresses, for the purpose of resisting the pressure of the masonry, forming the seats of the stadium on the side next the plain. The seats of the opposite side still remain.

All the buildings are constructed with the marble of the mountain, which in some instances assumes a dark hue, although the general tint is grey.

The whole circuit of the city walls may be easily traced descending from the acropolis to the plain; many masses remain worthy of admiration, for their solidity and beauty. There are also considerable remains of an inner wall of equal importance.

The city was approached by three gates: one of them is towards Kelibesh; beyond it are vaults and sepulchres hewn in the rock. Another is in the wall facing the plain, the descent to it is rugged and steep; the steps are continued beyond the gateway to a fountain, now surrounded by a marsh.

The site of Priene is entirely deserted; there are three mills and the house of a baker, at the foot of the mountain to the east of the city, at a spot now called Samsun; and beyond this the Turkish village of Kelibesh, consisting of about twelve houses. Higher up to the north of this is Giaur Kelibesh, a modern Greek village of about two hundred houses, in a flourishing condition, and daily increasing.

PLATE III.

VIEW OF THE TEMPLE OF MINERVA-POLIAS.

PLATE IV.

PLAN OF THE TEMPLE OF MINERVA-POLIAS.

The temple of Minerva-Polias, like most of the celebrated temples of Egypt and Greece, was surrounded by a peribolus, or cloister; the entrance to which was through a propylæum, or gateway. From the confusion in which the ruins lie heaped, the whole mass has been generally considered to have belonged to the temple only. A later and more minute investigation has demonstrated that some of the fragments attributed to the temple formed part of the propylæum.

The south wall of the peribolus, which is of rustic masonry, remains as high as the surface of the ground within, supporting a platform twenty feet in height. Part of the east wall adjoining the propylæum is still standing. Some vestiges extending in a straight line at a short distance from the south wall and parallel to it, lead us to infer that the peribolus was surrounded within by porticoes; in conformity with a custom very prevalent in Greece.

The plan of the temple is a parallelogram, one hundred and sixteen feet six inches long, by sixty four feet three inches, measured on the upper step. There were eleven columns in the flanks, and six in the fronts of the temple.

The walls of the cella ranged with the columns, which were second in order from those at the angles of the fronts, and inclosed an area of about sixty-five feet by thirty feet nine inches. They are four feet in thickness.

PLATE V.

ELEVATION OF THE TEMPLE.

This temple exhibits one of the few instances of Ionic columns with bases raised upon plinths. Although in buildings of Roman architecture plinths, and very frequently pedestals, are of common occurrence in such situations, their introduction has not been sanctioned by the practice of the Greeks: at least no building of an origin decidedly Grecian, erected in the best periods of the history of architecture, has been found to countenance the observance of such a mode of construction.

The propylæum, which we must consider as forming part of the grand edifice of the temple, exhibits a similar departure from the prevailing mode.

The columns are four feet three inches in diameter, and the intervals somewhat more than seven feet four inches, making the proportion of the interval to the diameter very nearly one and three-quarters to one. Had the ruins of this edifice been as inaccessible as those of the temple at Teos, described in the preceding chapter, the artist who travelled with Vitruvius for his architectural guide, would have concluded from the extent of the front, that the species of the temple was that termed Pycnostyle, by that author; supposing the usual intervals to have been nearly a diameter and a half of the columns, and the central interval larger. It is to such preconceived notions that the error in the ichnography of the temple of Teos, amongst other instances of similar arrangement, has arisen.

The shafts of the columns are composed of several frusta, a circumstance for which no probable reason can be assigned, as the marble of mount Mycale admitted of being quarried into blocks of considerable magnitude.

The capitals of the angular columns shew a similar face in both fronts. The doorway is given from conjecture.

PLATE VI.

THE ORDER OF THE COLUMNS.

A very considerable error occurred in the former edition of this work, in the representation of the bases of the columns; they are there shewn a foot less in diameter than the actual admeasurement gives them. The figured dimensions in the original drawings, which are preserved in the British Museum, are correct, the mistake has been made by the draughtsman.

The apparent want of substance in the base represented thus is wholly inconsistent with the principles followed by the architects of antiquity.

The base is formed by two blocks of marble, the lower being more than eleven inches and a half in depth, and the upper more than eight and a half. The torus is elliptical and fluted.

The eyes of the volute are bored two inches and a half in depth, perhaps for the convenience of fixing festoons of flowers, and the other apparatus with which the ancients were accustomed to adorn their temples on days of festivity, or public solemnity. The hem, or border, with its fillet, resting on the echinus, and connecting with a graceful sweep the spirals of the volutes, and in a manner keeping them fixed and secure in their place, adds greatly to the beauty of this capital.

PLATE VII.

THE CAPITAL AND BASE OF THE COLUMNS.

Fig. 1. The plinth and base, with the lower part of the shaft of the column.
Fig. 2. The capital and the fasciæ of the epistylium, with the upper part of the shaft of the column.

A specimen of the analogy between the capitals, bases, and lower part of the columns of these temples, has been given in the chapter on Teos.

PLATE VIII.

DETAILS OF THE ORDER.

Fig. 1. The plan of the capital, in which it is observable, the echinus is continued quite round, and appears with above half its projecture under the pillows of the volutes, contributing very much to its richness.

Fig. 2. An elevation of the profile of the capital.

Fig. 3. A section through the profile of the capital.

Fig. 4. A section through the front of the capital.

Fig. 5. The contour of the volute, of which the measures were collected not without much difficulty, it being necessary to have recourse to several different fragments.

The spiral of the volute has four revolutions, and may be described as follows. Let fall a perpendicular line, at pleasure, for the cathetus ; and set off from the point, whence it is dropped, any given distance for the centre of the eye, which being divided into six parts, the radius of the circle that describes the eye will be the half of one of them. To find the points, in which the centres of the spiral are fixed, draw two oblique lines, at the angle of forty-five degrees, through the centre of the eye ; then inscribe an hexagon, beginning at the intersection of the cathetus, with the upper part of the circumference of the eye, and divide the oblique lines, from the centre to their intersections with the sides of the hexagon, into three parts, which will give the points, in which the centres of the three first revolutions are fixed : for the fourth, bisect the remainder of the oblique lines between the centres of the third revolution, and the centre of the eye. Thus you will have the centres of the fourth revolution, and complete the spiral of the volute.

Fig. 6. A section through the torus of the base, in which the flutings and profile are distinctly marked.

PLATE IX.

DETAILS OF THE ENTABLATURE.

Fig. 1. The cornice of the temple.

The ornaments on the left hand of the lion's head are added, being the same as were found on the right.

It may be remarked, that the bottom of the sima does not spring from the edge of the fillet beneath, but leaves a small recess, which seems to indicate, that the materials of this member might originally be of lead ; for if a sheet of this be laid upon the cornice, and turned up in the form of a sima, (the use of which is to collect the water from the roof, and throw it off from the building, through the mouths of the lions' heads generally carved for that purpose),* it will naturally leave such a recess. This particularity is found in plain, as well as ornamental cornices, in the Greek buildings. Thus among others the PARTHENON, in the ACROPOLIS of ATHENS, has the cornice of the pediment crowned with an ovolo, which springs from the fillet beneath in the same manner, and has no ornaments.

A. The soffit of the dentils.

Fig. 2. A section through the cornice of the pediment, with its front annexed.

The ornaments on the sima are composed in a very different manner from those in the lateral cornice; and, lest this singularity should give reason to suspect an error in the application here, it is to be noted, that the measures of these two cornices were taken from an angular stone of the pediment.

Fig. 3. A section through the architrave of the temple, with its internal face.

The architrave was composed of three pieces, and the junction of the two lowermost was at the line marked in the section. The cymatium of the external face was the third; but we could find no remains of it. The compartment in the soffit has no ornaments in the pannel.

Fig. 4. A section through one of the transverse beams which supported the lacunaria, with one of its faces.

This also has a compartment in the soffit, like that of the architrave.

PLATE X.

THE ORNAMENTAL CORNICES.

The sima along the flanks of the temple was adorned with lions' heads, as described in the preceding plate. That of the pediment was ornamented in a manner altogether dissimilar. This cornice ends with the astragal below the echinus.

PLATE XI.

PLAN OF THE PROPYLÆUM.

All the temples of Egypt and Greece of any celebrity were surrounded by a peribolus. This was sometimes a wall, inclosing the court of the temple, but more frequently a peristyle, or open portico, with a propylæum or gateway in one of the ends.

The propylæum at Priene is a building of the Ionic order of architecture, having a tetrastyle portico in each front: within the principal portico is a door-way, of no considerable width, which gave access to the court and the temple beyond. The interior of the building is divided in width into three equal spaces, separated by two rows of Ionic pilasters, two feet each way: these are surmounted by capitals of a singular design, differing wholly, like all those of the pilasters of Grecian architecture, from the capitals of the columns. Like the interior columns of the Athenian propylæa, these pilasters support the marble cieling of the building and the roof, of the same material, above it.

The columns are more than two feet in diameter, and the intercolumniations are nearly five feet three inches in width, the intervals being to the diameter of the columns in the proportion of more than two and a half to one. The central interval is not enlarged in this instance, although, as we have already had occasion to remark, the severity of the rules applicable to the construction of sacred edifices, was sometimes disregarded in buildings of a less solemn character. According to the Grecian notions of beauty in architecture, the width of a portico bore some relation to the height, conjointly with some reference to the number of columns the front presented. Where there were only four columns in front the intervals were sometimes made equal to three times the diameter of the columns, whilst, on the other hand, in porticoes having ten columns in front, the intervals were sometimes a diameter and three-fourths, and sometimes, as in the instance of the temple of Apollo Didymæus, a diameter and six-tenths.

In a tetrastyle portico therefore there seemed to be little occasion for widening the central interval, unless when the dimensions of the building were altogether inconsiderable; when so much as three diameters of a column afforded an opening of insufficient width for the purposes of ingress.

PLATE XII.

THE PORTICO OF THE PROPYLÆUM.

The columns, like those of the temple, were raised upon plinths. The bases are of the common Attic form.

There are some features of the building indicating an age of architecture less pure than the period of the construction of the temple. The abacus of the capital has a fillet, a very unequivocal mark of degradation in architecture; the fasciæ of the epistylium are more unequally divided, and the frieze is less in depth, and without the cymatium or ovolo.

PLATE XIII.

TRANSVERSE SECTION OF THE PROPYLÆUM.

This section shows the insulated square pilasters supporting the lacunaria of the building. The beams, which extended longitudinally, are the only parts of the marble cieling which could be ascertained with precision. The other parts, and the carpentry of the roof, are conjectural. The epistylia, frieze, and cornice, are each in one block in thickness and depth; the gutta is hollowed in the top surface of the course forming the cornice in the flanks of the building.

A. Section of the joint tiles, in shape resembling half an hexagonal prism: they covered the junction of the flat tiles, and prevented the admission of water through the joints extending from the ridge to the gutter.

PLATE XIV.

THE FLANK OF THE PROPYLÆUM.

The walls in the flanks of the building were divided into compartments, by the introduction of two antæ of little projection. This is another departure from the purer style of the Greeks, who in a better age, would have left the wall plain between the two antæ terminating it.

PLATE XV.

THE ORDER OF THE COLUMNS.

Fig. 1. The base and capital of the columns.
Fig. 2. The soffit of the cornice, shewing the arrangement of the dentils.

PLATE XVI.

DETAILS OF THE ORDER.

Fig. 1. The flank of the capitals.
Fig. 2. Plan of the capitals.

Fig. 3. Section through the capitals, made by a plane passing through the front.
Fig. 4. Section through the capitals, made by a plane passing through the flanks.
Fig. 5. Section through the centre of the pulvinar, or cushion, of the capitals.
Fig. 6. Section of the cornice belonging to the pediments of the building.

PLATE XVII.

DETAILS OF THE ORNAMENTS.

Fig. 1. Capital and base of the insulated pilasters. Contrary to the practice observed in the purer specimens of Grecian architecture, the pilasters have a slight diminution from the bottom to the top.

Fig. 2. The ornament on the pulvinar of the capitals.

Fig. 3. The ornamental sima of the pediments.

Fig. 4. Section through one of the marble beams supporting the lacunaria.

Fig. 5. A fragment found amongst the ruins.

PLATE XVIII.

FRAGMENTS OF THE AGORA.

Fig. 1. A cornice found at some distance, to the south-east from the peribolus. The composition, proportion, and taste of the mouldings, agree perfectly well with the cornice of the peristyle,* and plainly prove, that it belonged to the same building, and, as the dentils are omitted, probably to a pediment in the front of the peribolus. The difference between the ornaments on the sima, and those of the cornice before mentioned, will offer no objection to this assumption, if it be remembered that those in the lateral cornice of the temple vary greatly from that in the pediment.†

Fig. 2. A Doric capital and entablature.

Below the temple, and contiguous to the south wall of the peribolus, is a large level piece of ground, of which the western end forms a terrace, faced with a rustic wall. The remnants of a Doric building, of white marble, are scattered over this spot, which, being situated in the centre of the city, is supposed to have been the site of the Agora.‡ Out of these fragments are collected this capital and entablature; but whether these members belonged to each other, cannot be ascertained. The measures are taken from stones lying separate, at such a distance as shews they were employed in very different parts of the building. However, on comparing the members together,

---

* See Pl. VIII. Fig. 6.
† See Pl. VI. Fig. 1 and 2.
‡ Ἀγορὰ ἐν quadrato, amplissimo et duplicibus porticibus, fora constituant, crebrioque columnis, et lapidibus aut marmoreis epistyliis adornant: et, supra ambulationes in contignationibus faciunt. Vitruv. L. v. c. 1.

no considerable disagreement is found in their proportions, except in the mutules, of which the length does not properly coincide with the breadth of the triglyphs. The sima was decorated with lions heads, which are defaced.

As not one of the shafts of the columns was entire, or in its place, neither their diameter nor altitude could be ascertained; but if two feet six inches and six-tenths be taken for the diameter, their diminution will be one-sixth; and if six diameters and a half for the altitude, the height of the entablature will be two-ninths and a half; but if steps are added to the columns, the height of the entablature may be made one-fourth, the steps included. The columns, in the portico erected by PHILIP of MACEDON at DELOS, and in the temple of JUPITER NEMEUS in ACHAIA,* have the same proportions. The height of the entablature in the former is three-elevenths of the column, which differs but very little from this. The example of the Doric portico at ATHENS is followed, in placing the capital and members of the entablature upon one another.

Fig. 3. The projection of the triglyph from the naked of the frieze.

* This temple is distant about five hours, a little to the south of west, from CORINTH, and one hour east from a village called St. GIORGIO.

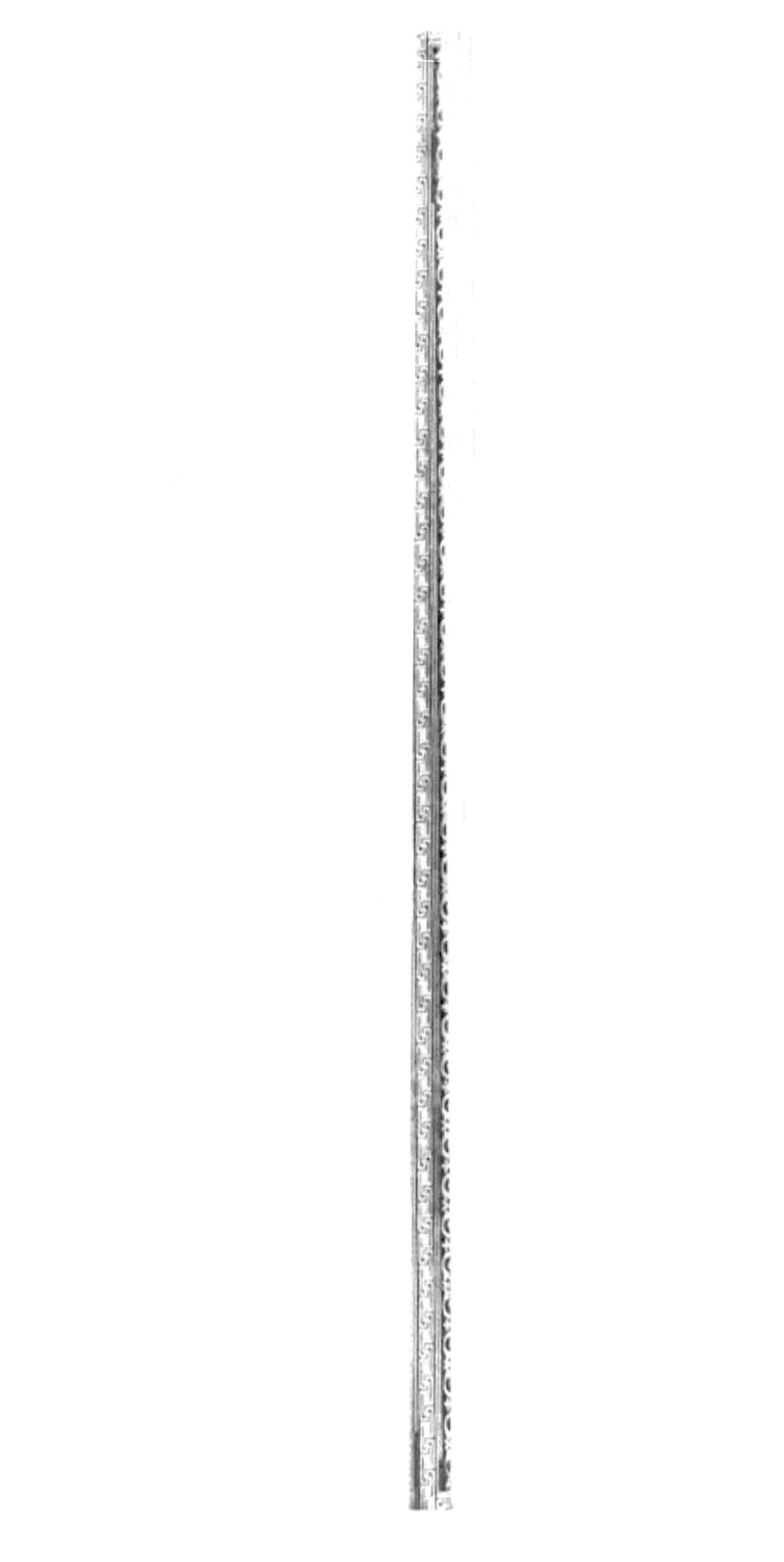

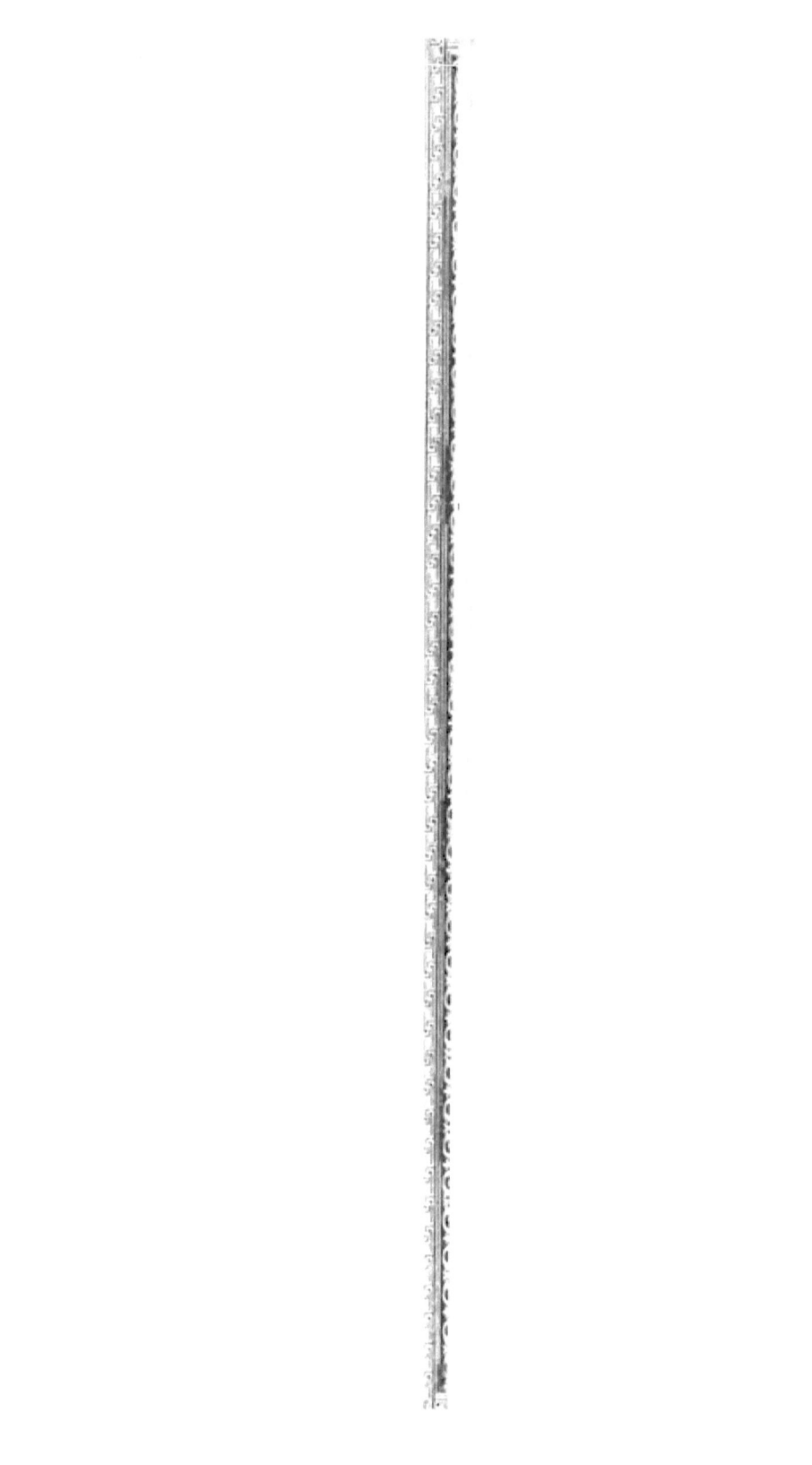

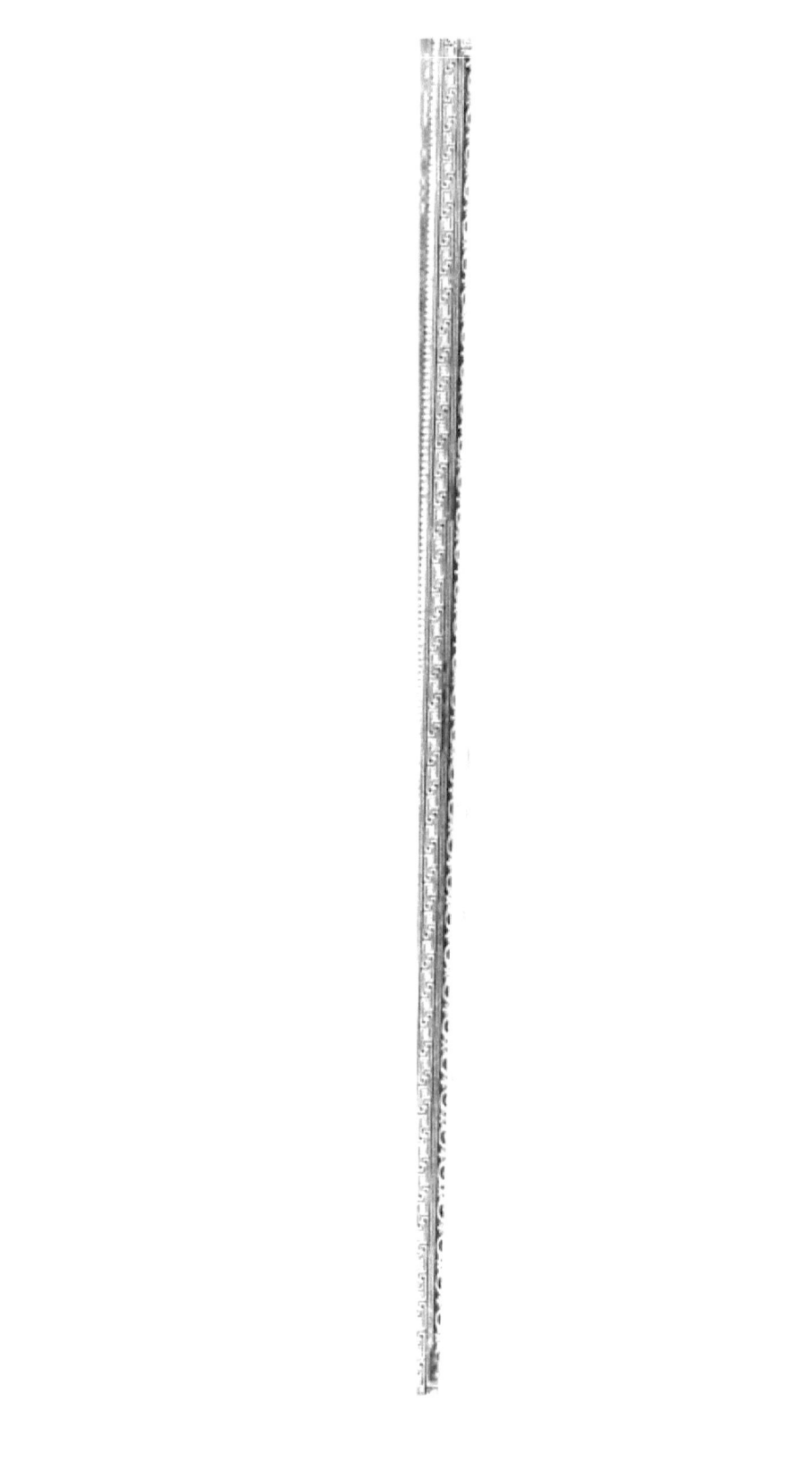

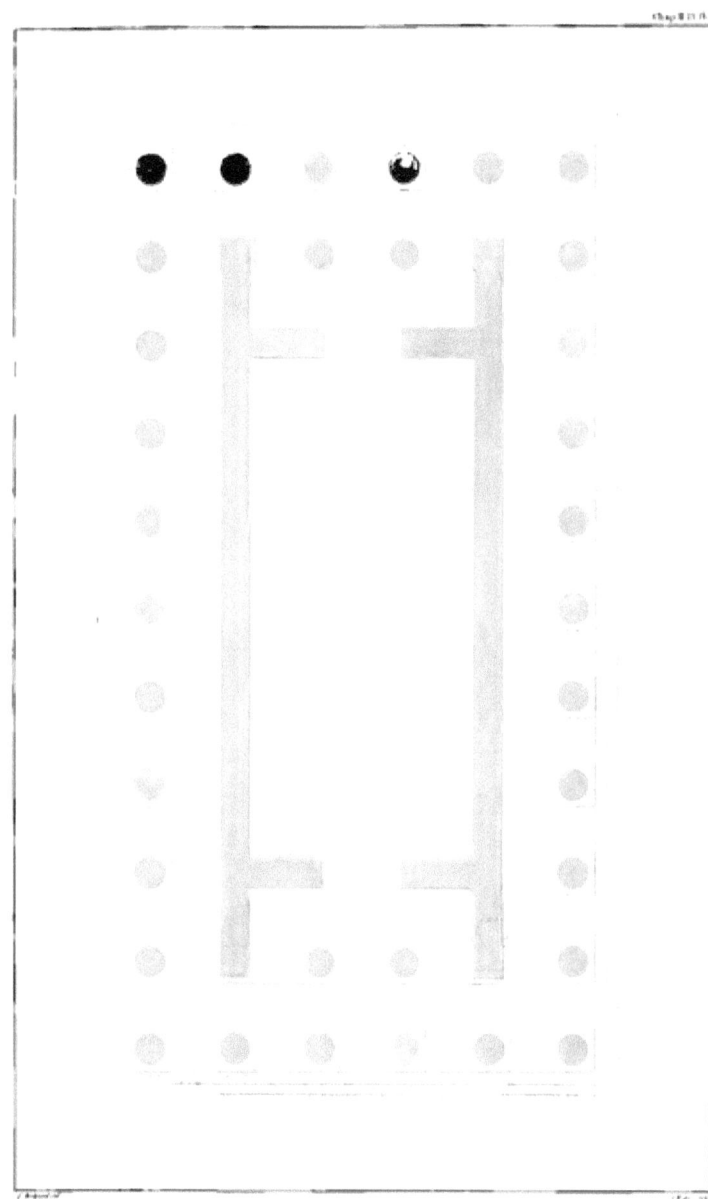

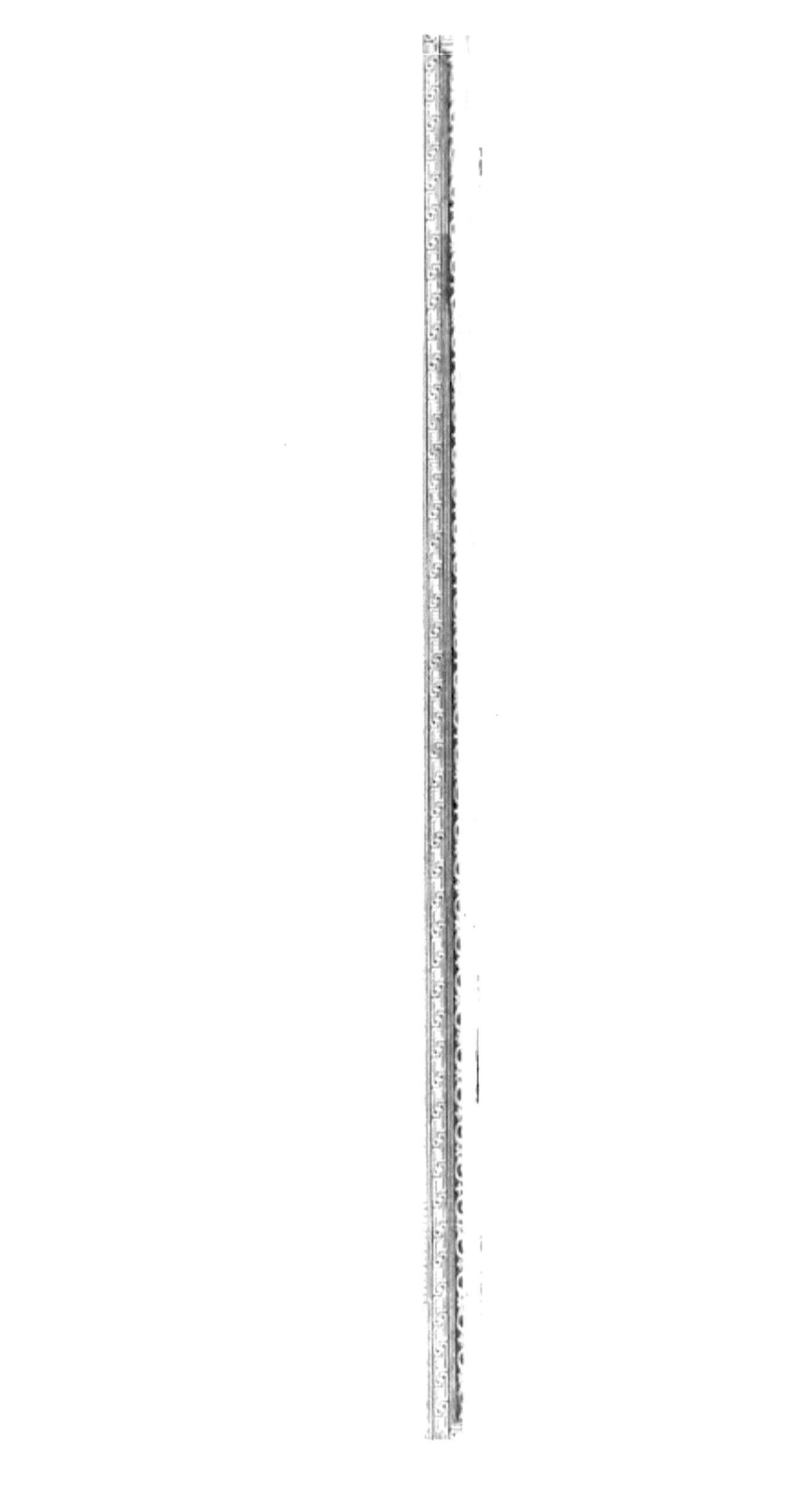

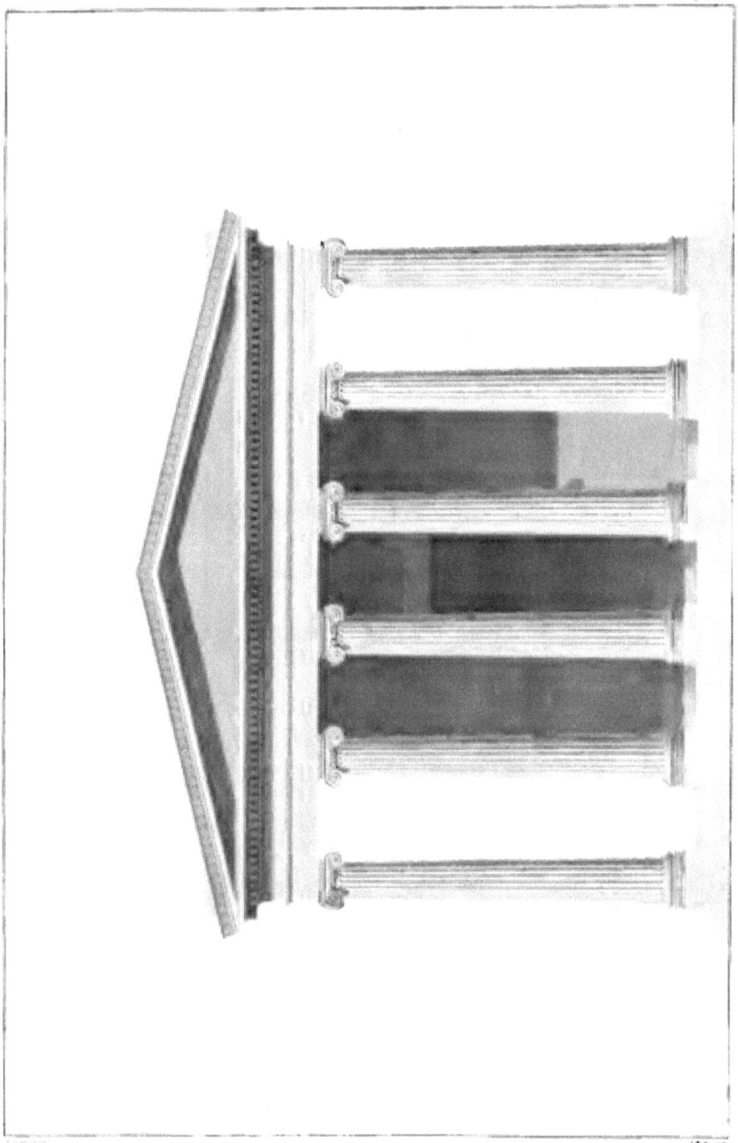

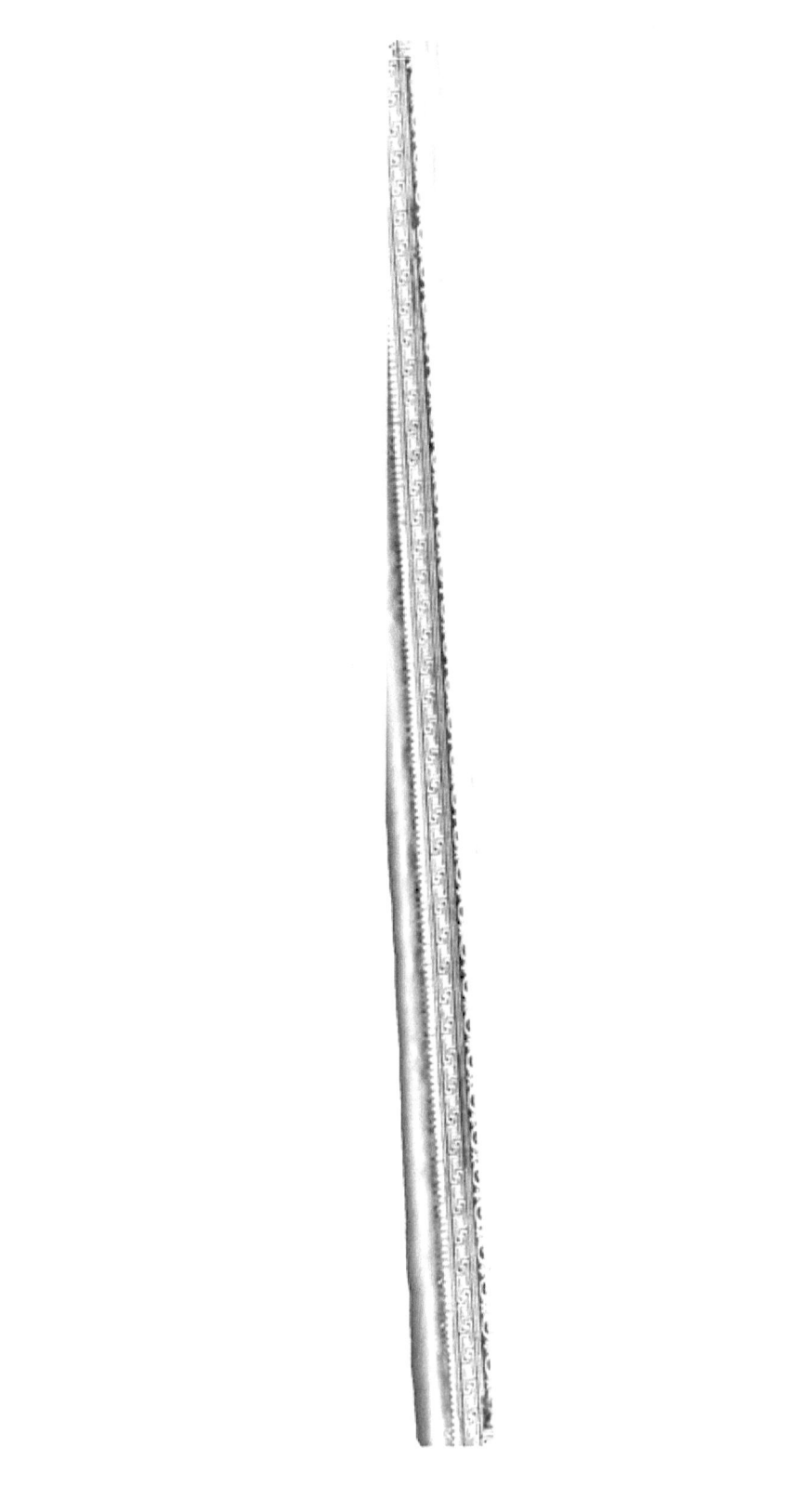

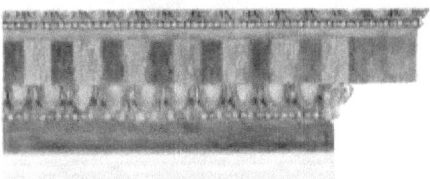

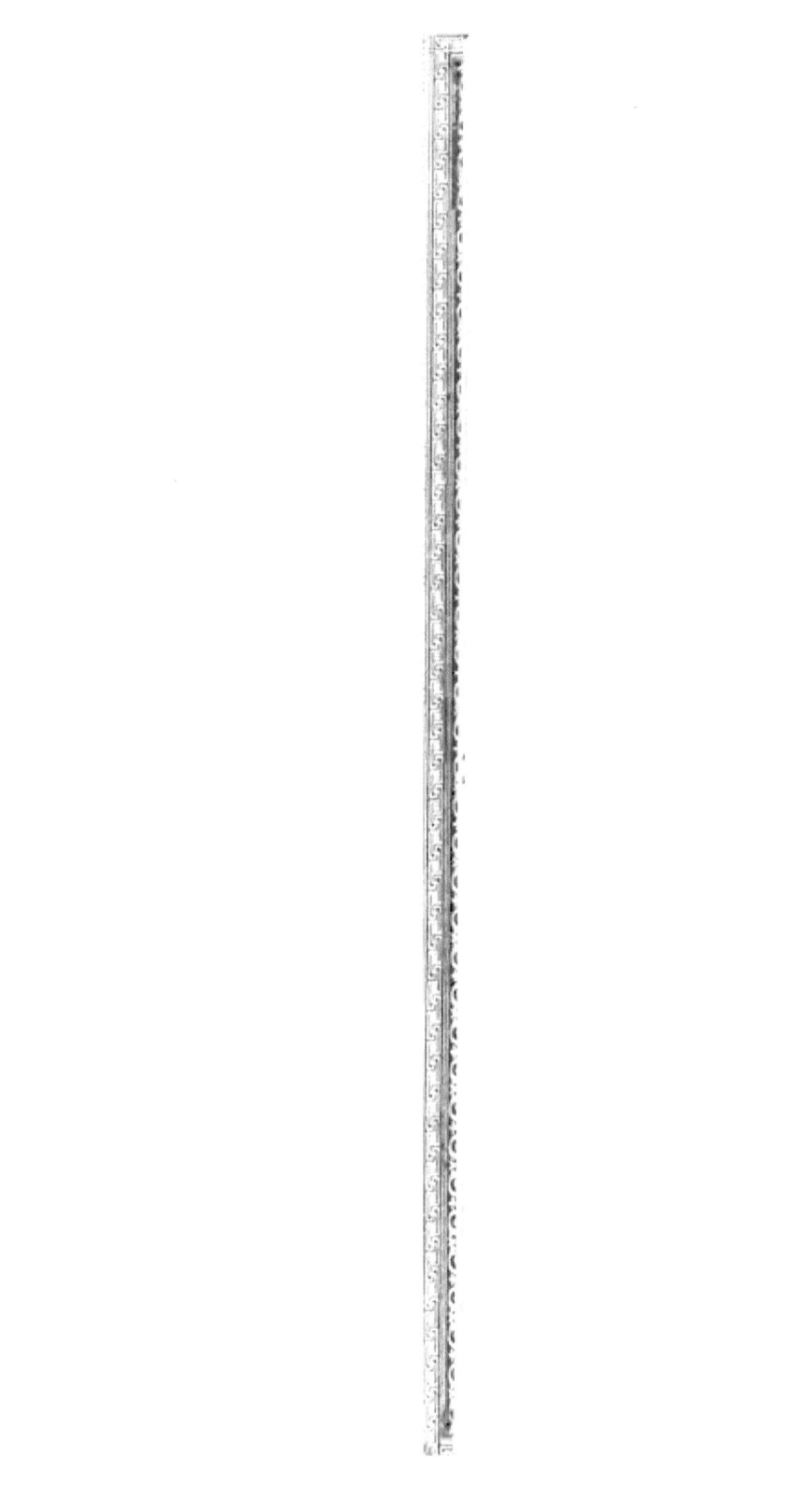

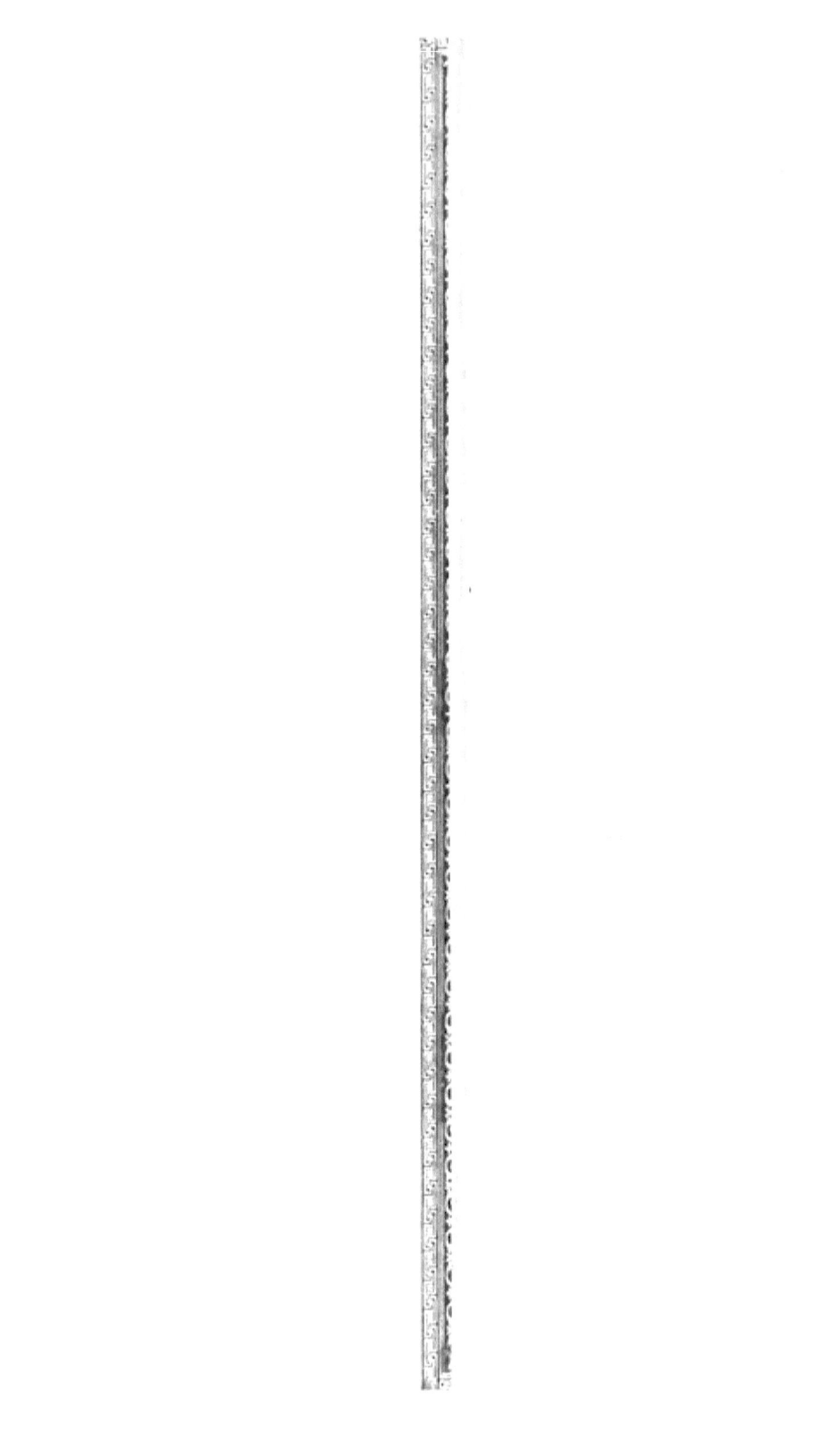

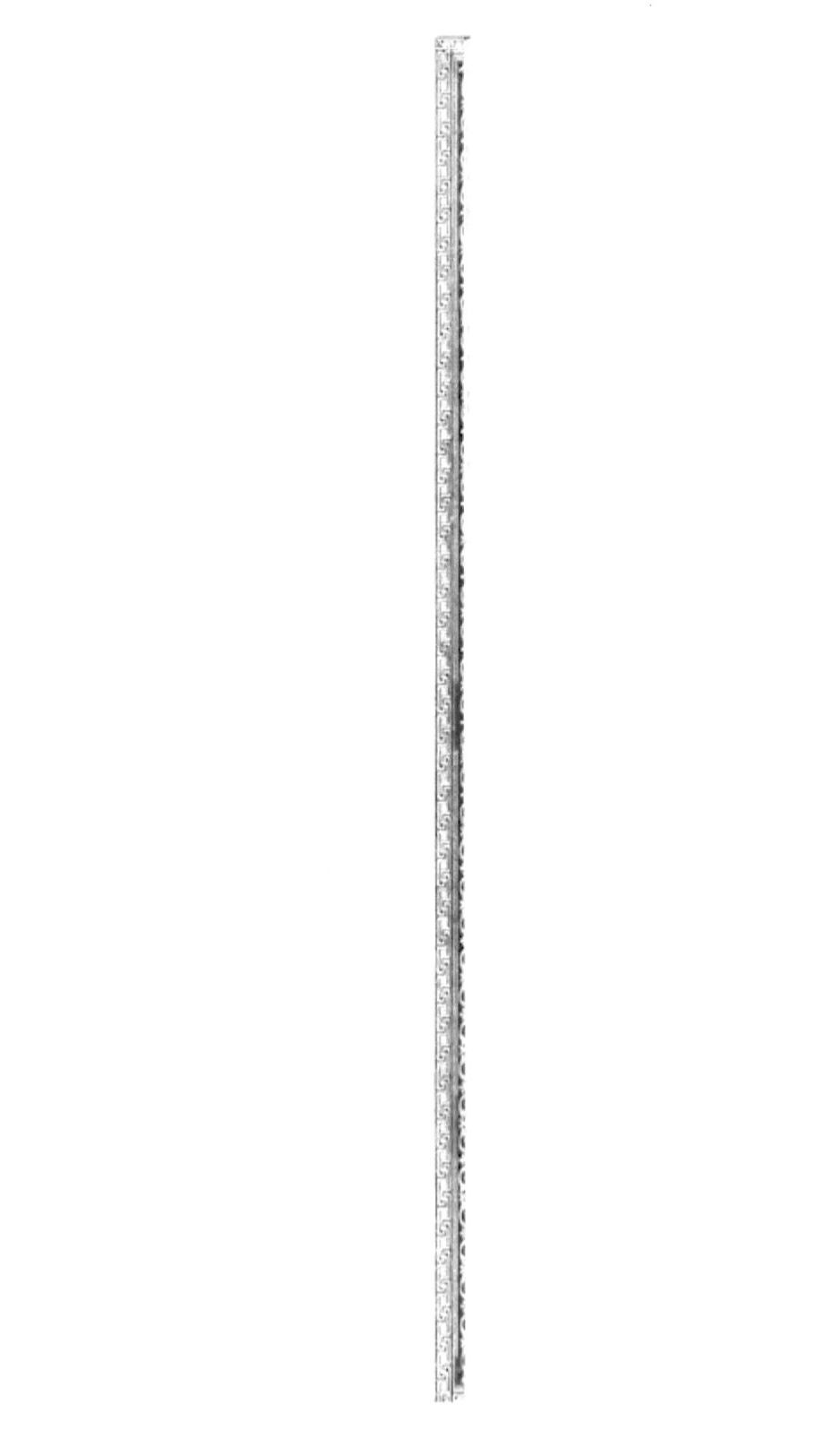

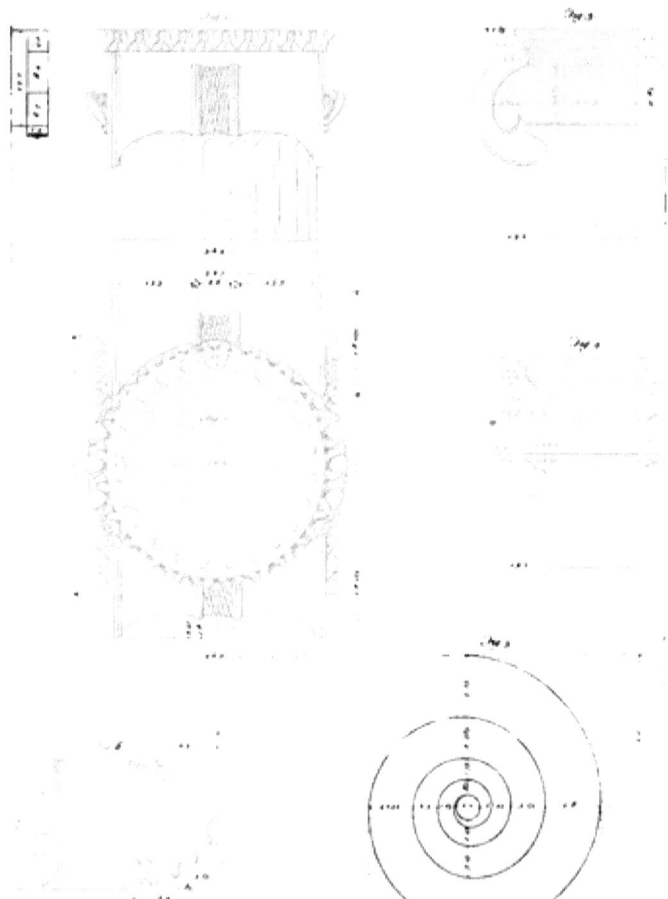

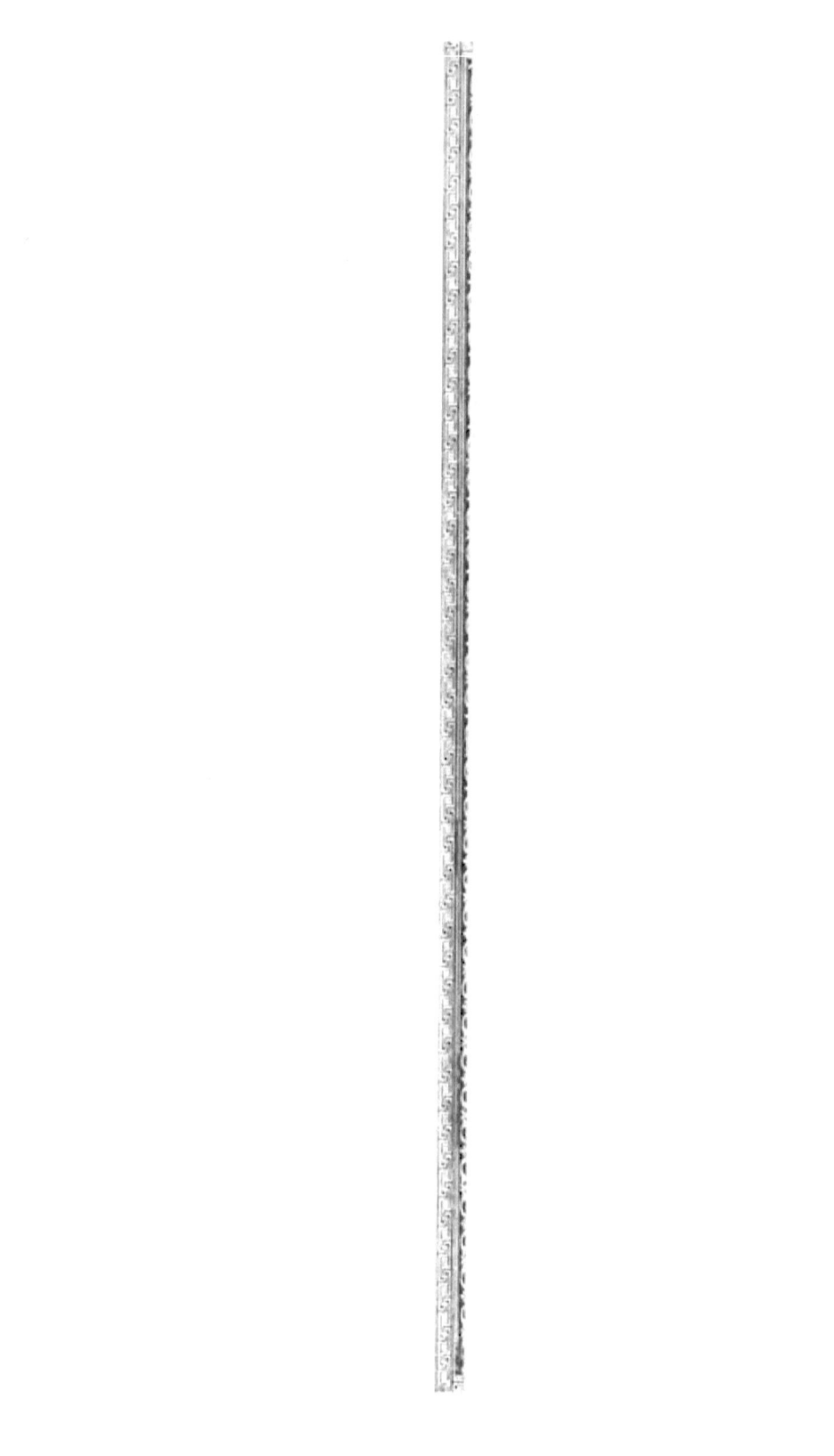

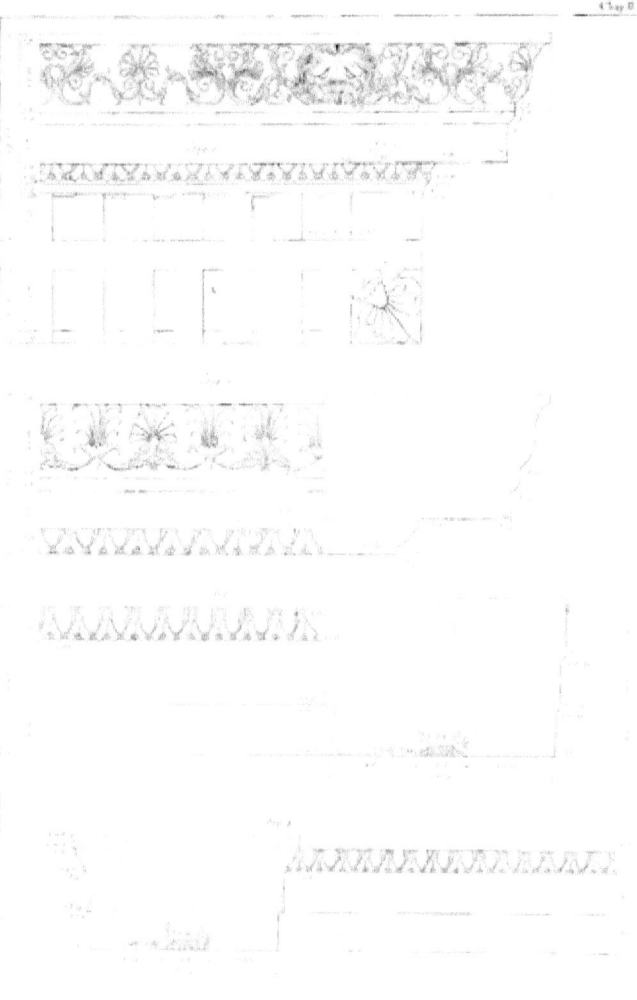

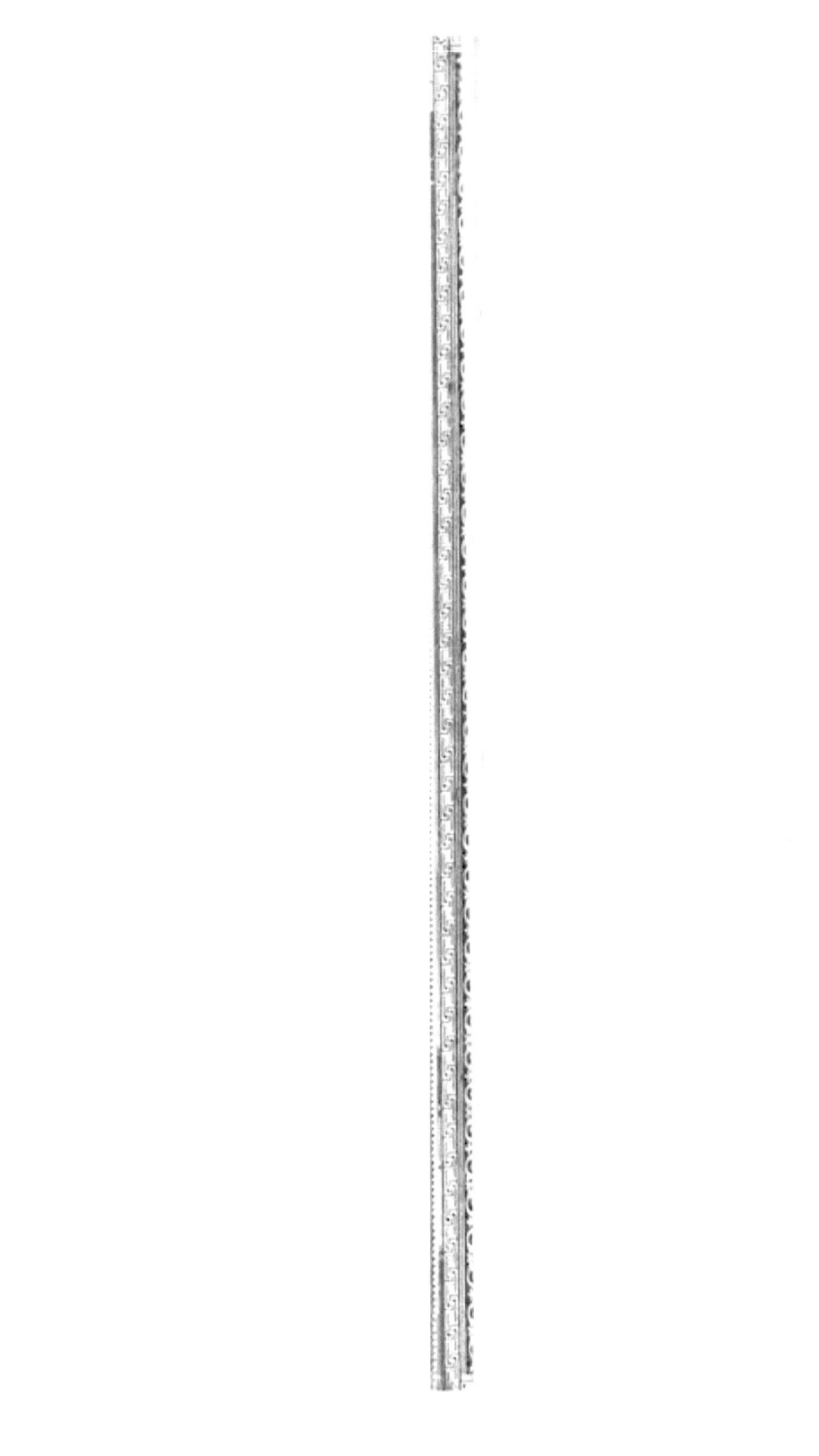

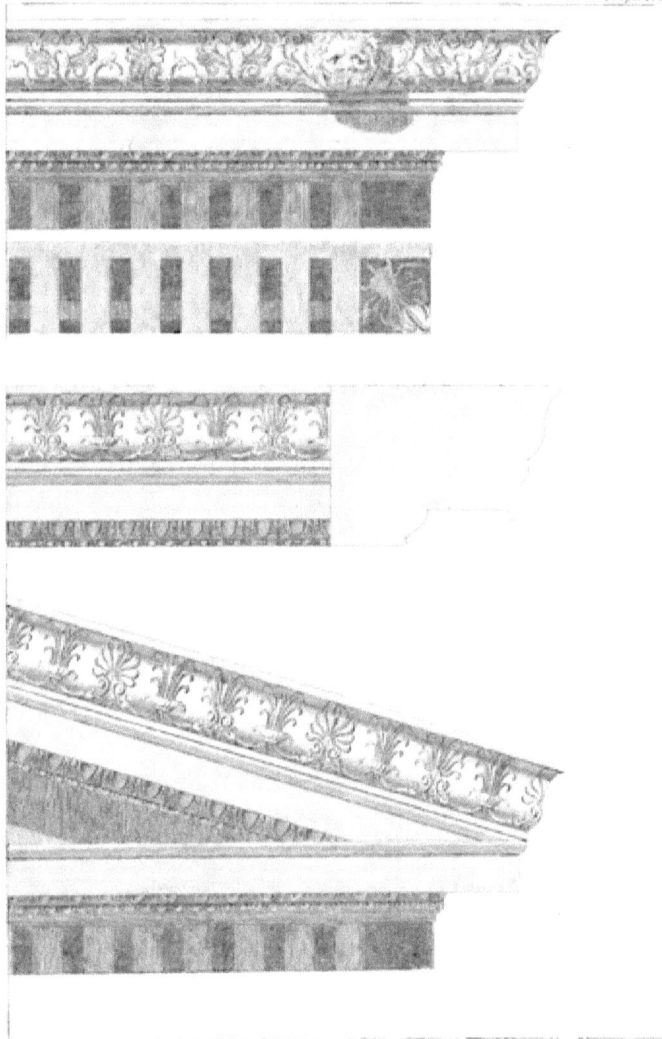

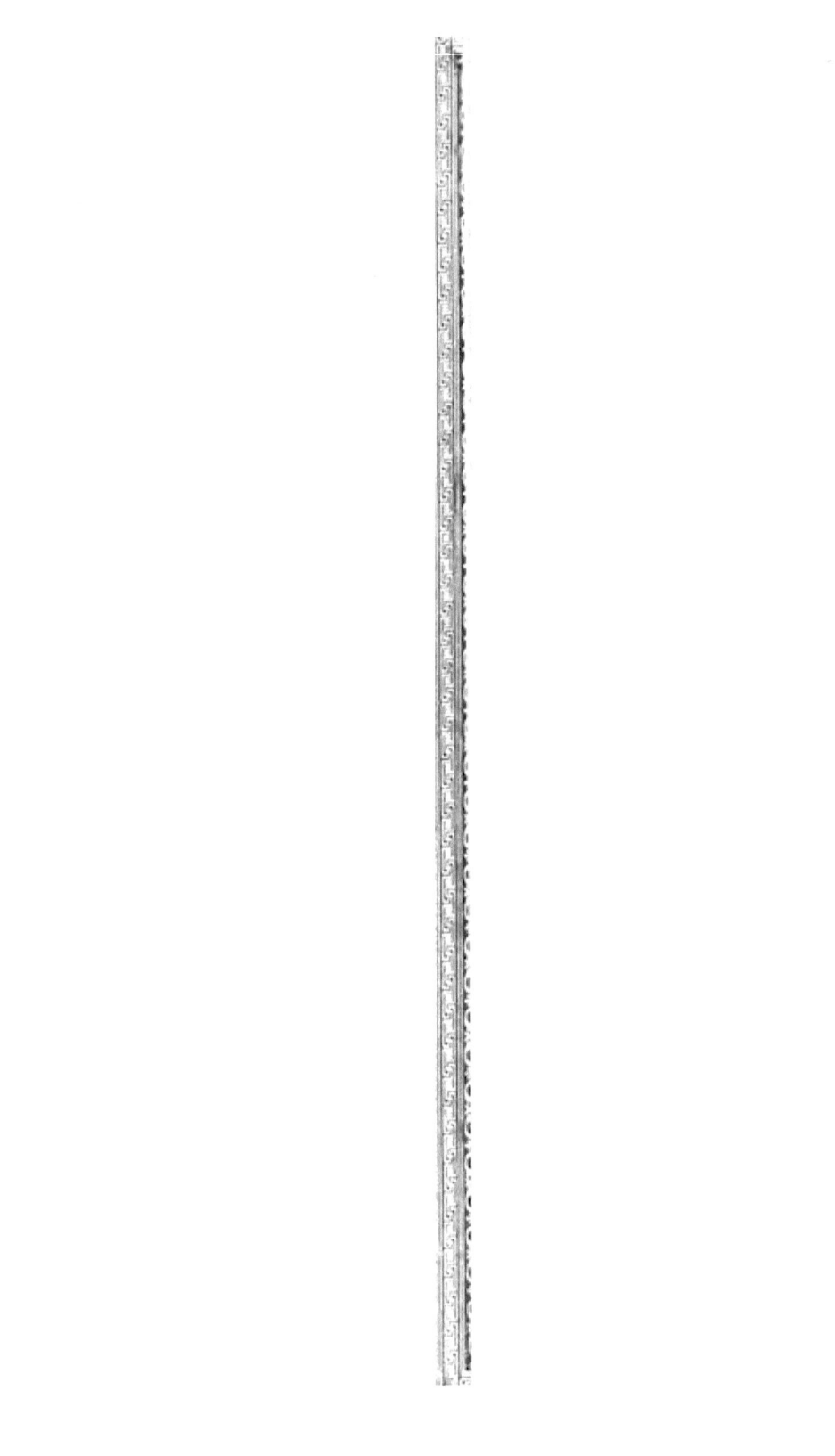

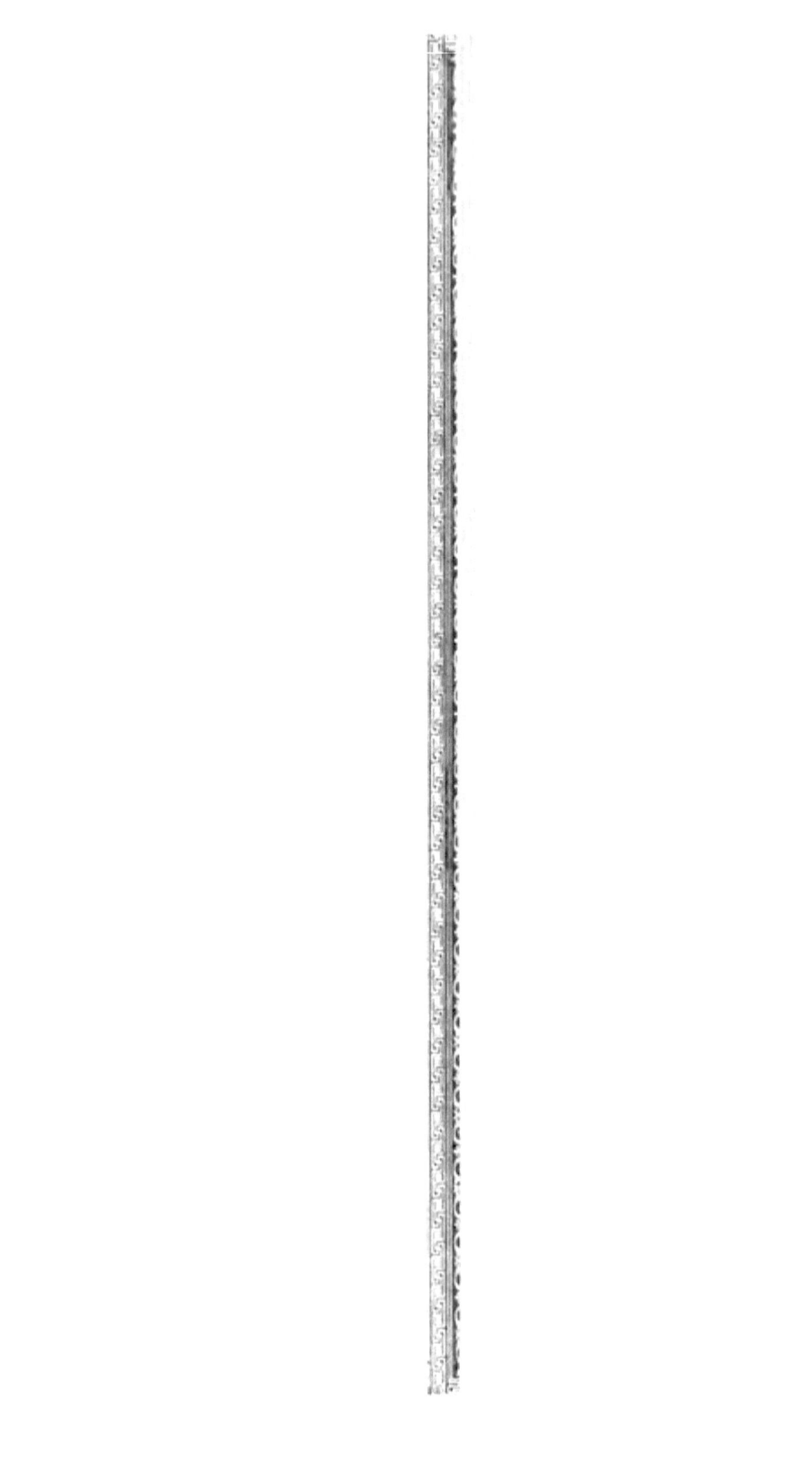

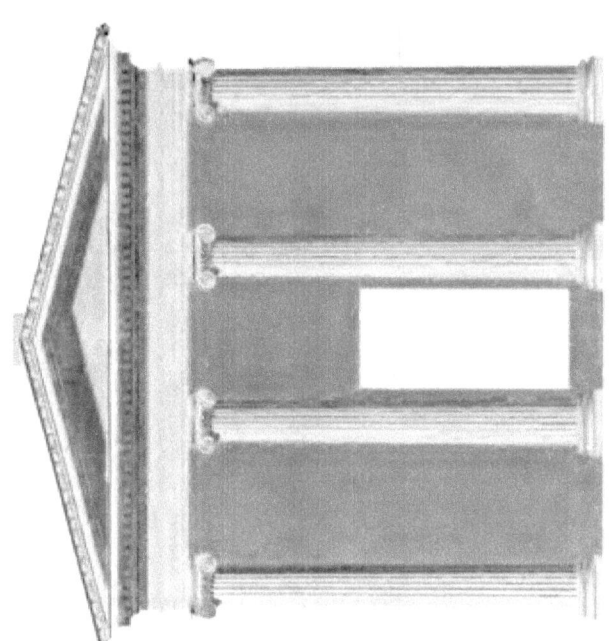

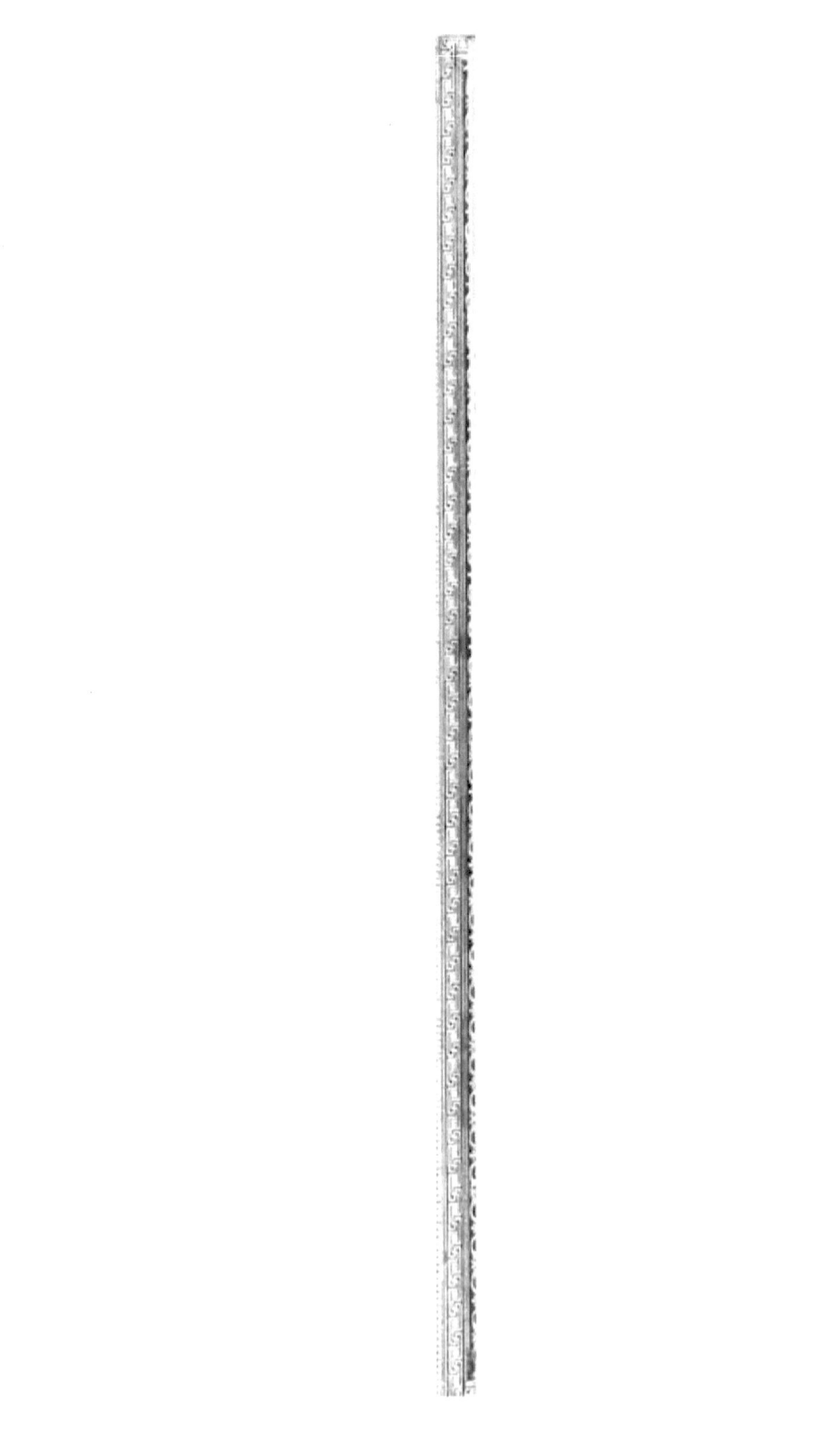

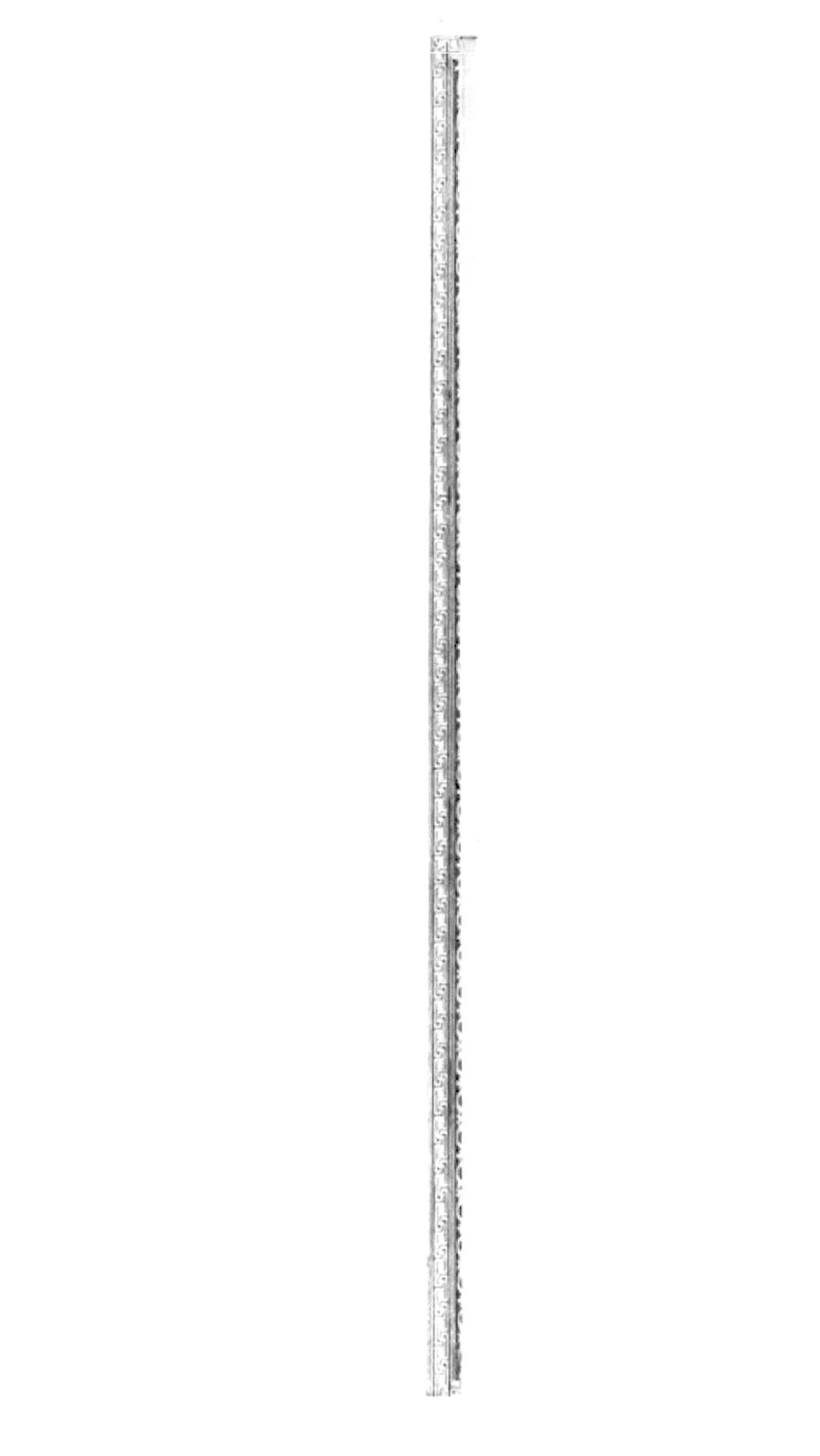

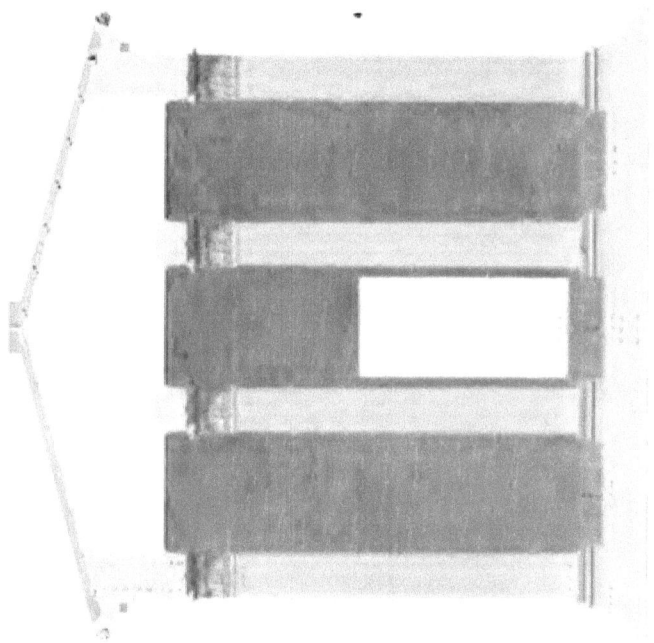

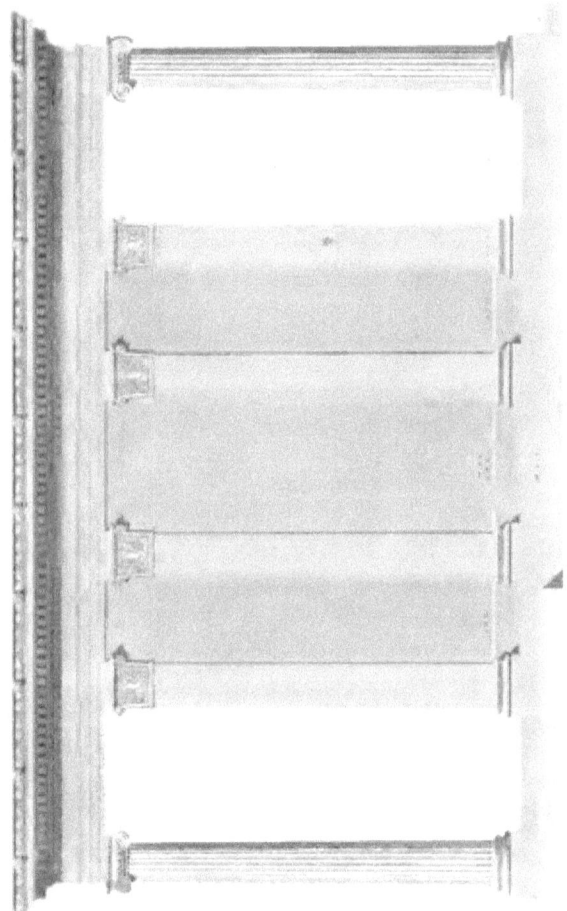

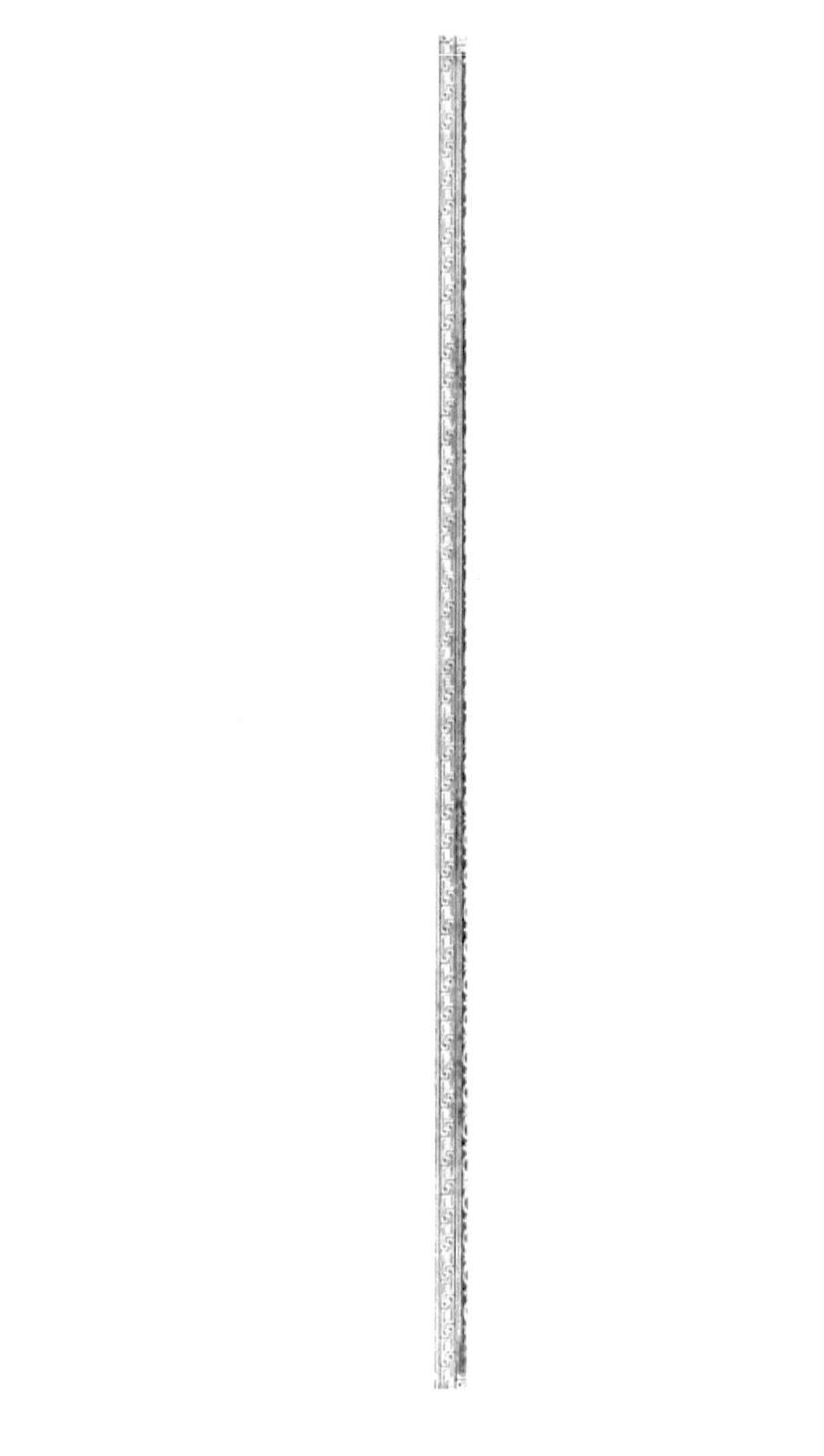

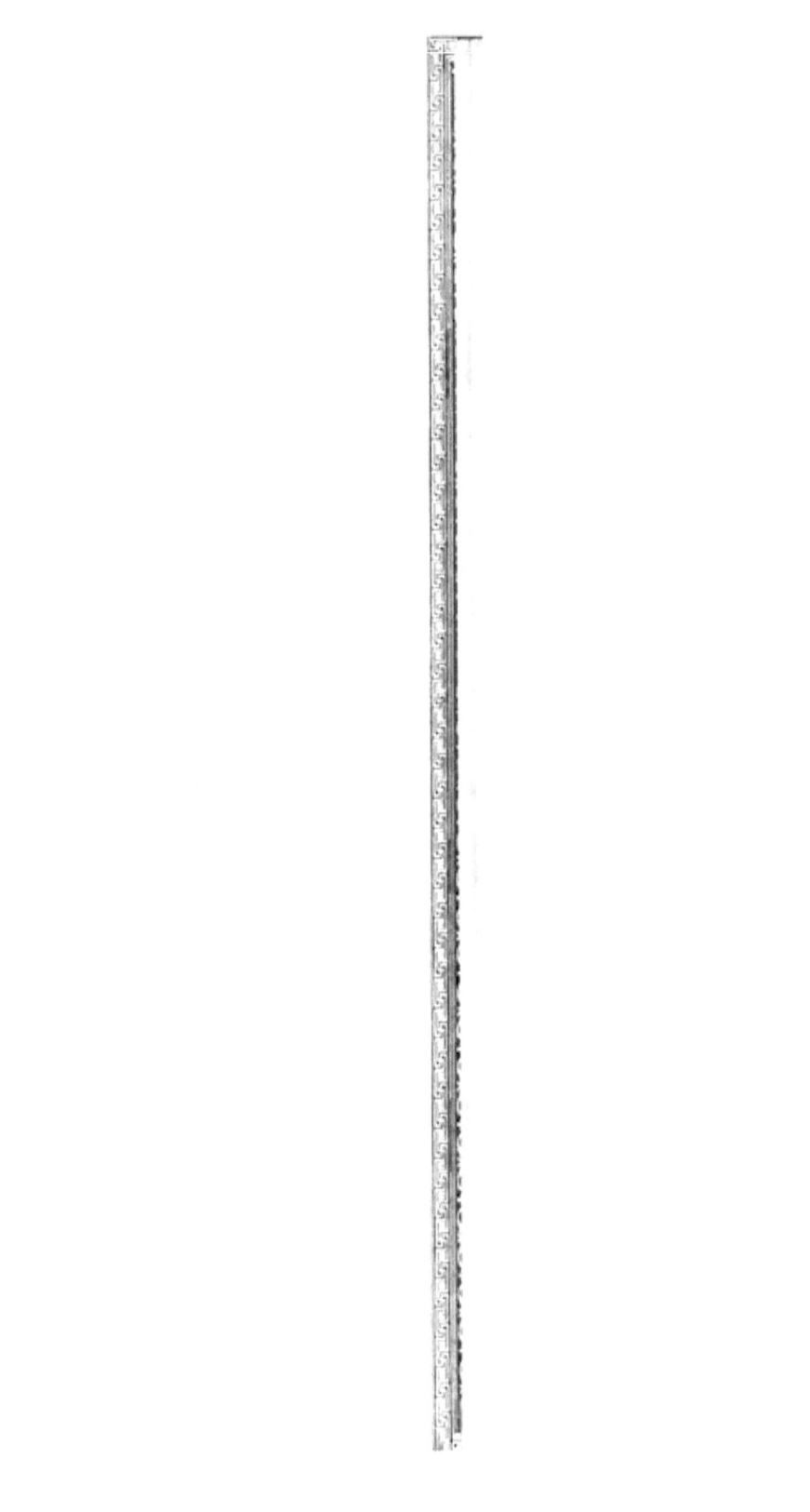

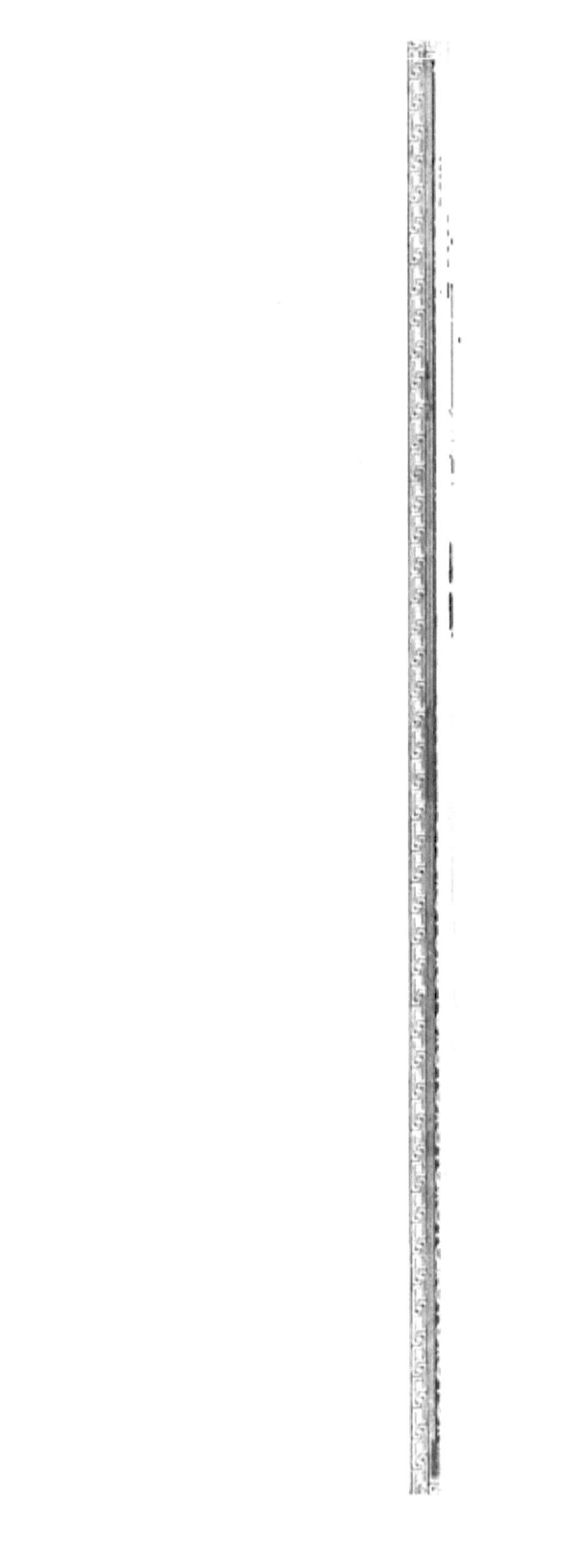

CHAPTER III

DIDYME.

The temple of the Branchidæ, or, as it was afterwards named, of Apollo Didymæus, with the Oracle, was not very remote either by sea or land from Miletus,[*] being seated on the promontory called Posideium, at the distance of eighteen or twenty stadia from the shore, and one hundred and eighty from the city;[†] and both are recorded as occupying this spot before the Ionic migration.[‡]

The appellation Branchidæ was derived from a very noted family so called, which continued in possession of the priesthood until the time of Xerxes, deducing its pedigree from the real or reputed founder and original proprietor, Branchus. Several of these sacred tribes flourished in Greece, and intermixed, as they did, fable with their genealogy, raising their progenitor, to conciliate a greater respect from the people, far above the level of common humanity. The story

---

[*] Strab. p. 634.
[†] Μέα δὲ τὰ Βρανχίδων τὸ Μιλησίων, οἷς τὸ τοῦ μαντεῖον τὰ ἀρχαῖον ἀπολέλειπε τε τὰ Βρανχίδαις, καταλαβ' ἅμα τοῖς πανδήμοις (Μιλ. πρίν τὰν Ἰωνικήν) ἐχόλασε. Ibid.
Oraculum a Posideio xviii. stad. Macrob. l. xvii.
Posideium Promontorium et oppidum Branchidarum appellatum, nunc Didymaei Apollinis, a littore stadiis viginti. Et inde centum octoginta, Miletus Ioniæ caput.—Plin. l. v. p. 227.
[‡] Pausan. l. vii. p. 525.

told by the Branchidæ is indeed sufficiently ridiculous; but if the repetition need an apology, it may be urged that one equally extravagant is the subject of a noble ode in Pindar,* written to commemorate the antiquity and renown of the prophetic family at Olympia, the once celebrated Iamidæ. It is related by Varro,† as follows.

A certain Olus, the tenth in descent from Apollo, after dining on the shore, renewed his journey, leaving behind his son Smicrus. The youth, thus forgotten, was received by one Patron, who set him to attend the goats, in company with his own two sons. These on a time catching a swan, and a dispute arising which should present it to their father, began to fight, covering the bird with a garment, which, when mutually tired, they removed, and discovered beneath it a woman. They were astonished, and would have fled, but she recalled them, and directed that Patron should prefer Smicrus to either. Accordingly, on hearing the tale, Patron caressed him with uncommon affection, and bestowed on him his daughter in marriage. She, during her pregnancy, beheld in a dream the sun passing down her throat, and through her body. Hence the infant was named Branchus, [ὁ βρογχος, the throat.] He, after kissing Apollo in the woods, was embraced by him, received a crown and wand, began to prophesy, and suddenly disappeared. The temple called the Branchiadon was erected to him, with other temples in honour of Apollo Philesius, ‡ and called Philesia, either from the kiss of Branchus, or the contest of the boys. §

Among the Milesian stories collected by Conon, one, as abridged by Photius, ‖ recorded, that Democlus, a Delphian, had a handsome son named Smicrus; that by command of the Oracle he sailed to Miletus, taking the lad with him, then aged thirteen; that, eager to reimbark, he, unwittingly, left him behind; that a son of Eritharses, a goatherd, led him sorrowing to his father; that Eritharses, informed of his family and misfortune, cherished him as his own

---

* Olymp. vi.

† Varro. Div. Rer. cited by the Scholiast on Statius, L. viii. v. 198.

‡ Φιλησιος, from φιλεω, *osculor*, because, as in the Greek narration of Conon, cited hereafter, φιλημα αὐτω παρεδω.

§ The dispute between the boys seems to have arisen from an equality in years, or their being δίδυμοι, *twins*; and from hence may be derived with probability the local names Δίδυμοι and Δίδυμα.

That title Διδυμαιος, given to Apollo, is very ancient:

Βακχε, και Διδυμευ, παιηχη, λοξια, αγυι. Orph. Hymn.

Και ὁ Διδυμευς δε ου μόνον το Ανακλωσιν των δύω, και τα εις το αυτο συναν Διδύμους σημαίνει. Lucian. Περι του Αστρολ. T. ii. p. 370.

Διδύμαιον Δελφινιον *vocant, quod geminam speciem sui ostentet (f. hominis) præfert; quæ illuminando formandoque homines cruentes ex uno forte locus geminos sidere dici et unctio illustrat.* Macrob. C. 17.

It is remarkable, that no mention of this Apollo is found in Homer or Pindar, unless in the hymns attributed to the former, v. 180. to Apoll.

'Ω Ανα —
Και Μιλητον εχεις, εναλον πολιν, ιμερόεσσαν.

‖ Ἡ λέγει. Ότι Δημοκλος ὁ Δελφος γενος παιδα ευπρεπη Σμικρον (f. Σμικρόν) τιγμα — τουτο αυτω χρησαντος του Απολλωνος, ἀγων σηματιωτα, εις τα Σωρου Αντιβακχου φιλα (f. Φιλεια) αφικνείται. Ὁ δε Βαγγιχος εξ Αντιβακχου επιστας αφικνείται γάμισας τε Δεμοκλος τω χρονω έτρεφε. Και αυχει ὡς τον βασιλέων Γαλαταιωσι, εν αγαστη μετα Δελφων, αφικεται ωσπερ ητο τε των Βραγχίδων. Conon. apud Photium, p. 112.

Branchum Thessalus fuit Apollini dilectus, et filius habitus, quem interfectum dolens, templo et divinitate sacravit. Lactant. Apollo Milesius claros — Clem. ab Alex. xi. 2.

Branchus quem ipse vaterperit, ex filia Iancris et Sucronis — et bonæ pater — mortuum communi templo sub veluti, cujus fecent sacerdos. Bulenard. Tractat. de Divinatione, p. 107.

Quem susceprit ex Iance Sucronis filia—ad superos reditus cui commune Milesiorum decretum—unde ipse Deus Branchides appellatus est. p. 136.

patriisque aequalis honori
Branchum—Statius, L. iii. v. 479.

*et lacessit clabyt penetralia Branchi,
Nec Claria* hac luce fovet, Didymaeaque quinquere
Lumina, nec Lycium supplex consulitur adibit.

L. viii. ver. 198.

offspring; also concerning the swan, the contention of the two boys, and the appearance of Leucothea; and that she bade them command the Milesians to honour her, and to celebrate a gymnic agon of boys, for she had been delighted with their contest; that Smicrus married the daughter of a principal Milesian; that she saw the vision before described, which was interpreted by the prophets to be a good one; that the child was named from it, and became the most beautiful of men; that Apollo, finding him feeding his flock, was enamoured with, and kissed him, upon the spot on which an altar dedicated to him was afterwards placed; that Branchus was inspired by him, and prophesied at Didymi, where the Oracle of the Branchidæ was still confessedly the prime throughout Greece, excepting only the Delphic. It is likely the agon believed to be instituted to gratify this imaginary Leucothea, was one of the Didymæan games, which continued to be solemnized at Miletus for many centuries."

This account will, it may be presumed, fully satisfy even the most curious in ancient legends, as to the fables about Branchus, and the love of Apollo mentioned, as current here, by Strabo;† who moreover reports, that at Delphi, Branchus was affirmed to be descended from the Delphian, by whom Neoptolemus, the son of Achilles, was slain.‡ The occasion of this bloodshed is differently represented; but the geographer conjectures the true motive was, that Neoptolemus had a design on the temple, of which the immense wealth was become proverbial even before the Trojan war.§

The ceremonial of a lustration performed by the prophet Branchus on the Milesians after a plague, was as follows: he sprinkled the multitude with laurel branches, and began a hymn,

Μέλπετε, ὦ παῖδες, Ἕκαεργον καὶ Ἑκαέργαν.
Sing, boys, Apollo and Diana.¶

To which exhortation they replied in certain hard and enigmatical words, like those used at the dismission from the Eleusinian mysteries.*'*

While he presided over the temple and Oracle, the Milesians were divided between Leodamas and Phitres, two of the regal line, contending with each other for the dominion. The community, wearied with faction, decreed, he should govern who proved the greatest benefactor to the public. Phitres returned unsuccessful from the war allotted to him; but Leodamas overcame the Carystians, and took their city. On his arrival at Miletus, he sent to Branchidæ, as the

---

* ΜΗΛΕΙΩΝ ΔΙΔΥΜΕΙΑ. Muson. Oxon.
† Ἑλαυδω δὲ μίλετοι καὶ τὸ περὶ τὸν Βραγχον, καὶ τὸν τοῦ παῖδα τὸν Ἀπολλωνος. Strab. p. 633.
‡ Strab. p. 421. See also Meursh, Tryphiod. p. 133.
§ Oὐχ᾽ ἵνα λαϐοι τάδε αφαίρεσιν τοῦς τυφως Φοῖβε Ἀπολλωνος. Homer.
Clemens Alex. p. 674.
¶ Macnedrios (C. Leandrios) scribit Milesios Antiochum Osten pro salute sua immolare. Pherecydes refert, Thesea, cum in Cretam ad Minotaurum duceretur, vovisse pro salute et reditu suo Antiochum Osten ab Apolline Delio. Macrob. l. i. c. 17.

Strabo also mentions, that the Milesians invoked Apollo by the title Ulios, as god of health. P. 635.
Apollo Didymæus, on a Milesian medal, holds in his right hand the image of Diana; on others, as is sometimes seen above; and on many, joined, as in the Address of Branchus, with her brother.
'* Potter, V. i. p. 391, 393.

Oracle had commanded, a captive woman with a child at her breast, and many other offerings, the tenth of the spoils. The woman was much esteemed by Branchus, who adopted her son. The boy grew up, as favoured by some divinity, and possessed an understanding superior to his years. He was appointed to be the bearer of the prophecies, and named Evangelus (*The good Messenger*) by Branchus, whom he succeeded* in his office. He was the founder of the Milesian family, called from him the Evangelidæ.

It may be remarked here, that though some other deities were also regarded as prophetic, Apollo was principally renowned for the frequent use of this talent. Hence he is distinguished by the sly derider, Lucian,† as one of the many divinities, whose lot was far from being so easy and happy, as Homer had represented; for, says Jupiter, " undertaking a very troublesome occu-
" pation, he is almost deafened by the multitudes crowding to consult him. Now he must be at
" Delphi, soon after he hurries to Colophon, then away to the Xanthus, then runs to Claros,
" then to Delos or the Branchidæ; in fine, wherever a prophetess, after drinking from the
" sacred fountain, chewing laurel, and shaking the tripod, commands him to be present, it behoves
" him instantly to attend with his responses ready, or he will be undone." This multiplicity of business requiring order as well as dispatch, the god had stated times of audience and reply at the Oracles to which he belonged; being regularly in waiting on fixed days and hours, at particular seasons, when at his own option; for instances remain, in which he was forcibly compelled to exercise his faculty, in compliance with appellants too rude, irreverent, and boisterous, to admit the civil excuse either of his indisposition or absence.

But omitting the supposed agency of his fictitious godship, it is probable that Branchus, before he crossed over to Miletus, had been initiated into the mysteries of the gainful craft so successfully established in his native country; and as the juggle introduced by him strongly resembles that practised at Delphi and other oracular temples of Apollo, it is not unlikely that a mutual consciousness and intelligence subsisted between their respective managers.

The mode of consultation instituted here was attended, besides expense, with much ceremony and delay; the former adopted to give solemnity, the latter contrived to gain time for consideration, and to prepare the answer. The prophetess indeed appears to have sustained a very unpleasant character in the farce, if, with her bathing, she really fasted, as was asserted, for three entire days: At length, the previous rites being ended, she, bearing the wand given by the god, was believed to be filled with divine light; foretold futurity, sitting on the axle of a wheel; or received the Deity, while enveloped in the steam arising from the fountain; or on dipping her feet, or a certain hem of her garment, into the water. Possessed and solaced by this inward light, she tarried a long while in the sanctuary. The expecting votary propounded the question to be resolved, and the god was feigned to vouchsafe utterance through the organs of the inflated female.

Apollo, both at Branchidæ and Delphi, displayed his prescience verbally. The talent of extemporary versification was supposed to be derived from him, and the Pythia for many ages gave her responses in verse; but profane jesters affirming, that of all poets the god of poesy was the most wretched, she consulted his credit by condescending to use prose; and these replies were converted into metre by bards * serving in the temple. From the specimens yet extant, we may safely pronounce the genius of the god to have been as contemptible in Asia as in Greece, disgracing in both the heroic measure,† the chief vehicle of his predictions; and there likewise he seems to have retreated behind a substitute; for, in an inscription ‡ relating to this temple, we find the prophet and poet recorded as distinct persons.

That he acquired a very early and extensive reputation at Branchidæ, is evinced by ancient history.

When Necho, King of Egypt, had obtained a victory over the Syrians, followed by the capture of a great city, he would not change his raiment before he had consecrated a portion of the spoils to Apollo, and transmitted them thither.§

Crœsus, when he meditated to invade Cyrus, and consulted the Oracles, did not omit this.‖ The answer only of the Delphic was remembered when Herodotus wrote;¶ but the king, profusely munificent on that occasion, dedicated his choicest treasure, sending thither, as Herodotus was informed,** similar gifts and equal in weight to those he consigned to Delphi.

[illegible] Iamblichus, c. xi.

[illegible] Origen contra Celsum, p. 33, edit. Cant.

* Strab. L. ix. p. 419.

† Herum efficit versus interrogationibus consonos, ad numeros et modos plene concinnos: quales leguntur Pythici, vel ex oraculis editi Branchidarum. Marcellin. L. xxix. c. 1.

> Nexum et stemma petitur quater his repetitis,
> Hymnum Battiadem Phœbo cantare Delique,
> Prosarum Branchidarum quam duplex acumen pinxit
> Fatidicus sortes chordis depromere Pæan.
>
> Terentian. de Metris, v. 165. Hexametrum, apud Poetas Latin. V. ii. p. 1250.

‡ Chish. p. 91.

§ He reigned ante Ch. 616. Herod. L. ii. c. 159.

‖ Ante Ch. 549. Herod. L. i. c. 46.

¶ Herod. L. i. c. 47.

** Herod. L. i. c. 92. A Catalogue of the Delphic Offerings may be found, L. i. c. 50, 51, 52, with the weight of several, which, being reduced to the English standard, will give in part the value of those dedicated here. Another of his offerings is recorded L. i. c. 92. And see Strabo concerning the Delphic treasury, p. 420.

In the following anecdote, indeed, our god appears with far less dignity and importance. Pactyas had induced the Lydians to revolt from Cyrus, but fled, on the approach of an army, to Cyme. The general demanding the fugitive, the Cymæans demurred, resolving first to consult this Oracle, even then very ancient, and commonly frequented by the Ionians and Æolians. The messengers, asking what conduct with regard to Pactyas would be most pleasing to the gods, were answered, " a compliance with the Persian." The multitude, on their return, was disposed to obey; but Aristodicus, a principal citizen, prevented it, until the response should be confirmed. Aristodicus now went, and propounded the question, " O King, Pactyas a Lydian, dreading a " violent death from the Persians, fled to the Cymæans, who are required to surrender him back; " but we, though in awe of the Persian power, yet have feared to do it, until we obtain undoubted " counsel from thee." Aristodicus was displeased with the reply, and going round about the temple, as he had predetermined, seized the sparrows and birds from their nests, when a voice, it was said, reached him from the sanctuary, " Most impious of men! how darest thou to plunder " the suppliants from my temple?" But he replied, " O king! dost thou interpose for these sup-" pliants, and yet command the Cymæans to deliver up that suppliant?" It was answered, " Yes, " that for your impiety ye may speedily perish, nor come again to the Oracle on such business." This dialogue being reported, the Cymæans sent away Pactyas to Mytilene, in order to avoid the divine vengeance, which, it was supposed, would attend the giving him up; or a siege, which, it was apprehended, would be the consequence of detaining him.

The treasure consecrated by Crœsus was so considerable, that when Histiæus, by a messenger from Susa, advised the Milesians to revolt from the Persians, all were willing. Hecatæus, the historian, after enumerating the nations over which Darius ruled, enlarging on his power, and dissuading them without effect, counselled, that they should endeavour to secure the dominion of the sea, which, as their naval power was weak, he saw no method of attaining, unless by applying these riches of the temple to that end; a measure, from which he hoped much, besides the supplying their necessities and depriving the enemy of such valuable pillage: but the proposal was rejected.

The Persians, under Xerxes the son of Darius, afterwards despoiled the temple and Oracle of all their wealth, setting fire to this and the other temples, except at Ephesus, and urging, as an example, the treatment which Sardis had experienced from the Ionians, when in their possession. This monarch was particularly angry with the Milesians, believing they had behaved ill designedly in the sea engagement with the Athenians at Salamis.

The Branchidæ, who sided with the Persians, became on his misscarriage the voluntary companions of his flight, to avoid the punishment due to their treachery and sacrilege.

DIDYME. 55

It is likely the Milesians were too much impoverished and depressed to attempt directly the restoration of their temple; nor is it certain when they began to rear the fabric now in ruins. But the architects were Peonius, an Ephesian, and Daphnis of Miletus. The former, with Demetrius, a servant of Diana, was said to have completed her temple at Ephesus, which also was of the Ionic order, and had been planned, but not finished, by Ctesiphon the Cnossian, and his son Metagenes, the authors of a treatise on it.

The age in which Peonius flourished, some perhaps will imagine, may be discovered from the history of the Ephesian temple. But it should be remembered, the edifice he completed was that which was begun, or intended in the reign of Crœsus; for many of the pillars were presented by him; this being the temple which rose on the contribution of all Asia, and was two hundred years about; as also, that spared by Xerxes, and of which Strabo declares, Chersiphron was the original architect, that it was enlarged by another person, and finally burned by Herostratus. This event happened on the night when Alexander was born. The Ephesians displayed great zeal for its immediate restoration, selling the old pillars, and bestowing even the ornaments of female dress, to render it superior in magnificence to the other; and this was the structure of which Alexander offered to defray the whole expense for the honour of inscribing it. The architect was the famous projector who proposed to Alexander, after perfecting this temple, to form Mount Athos into a statue of him, in the attitude of making a libation, with a river issuing from a beaker in one hand, running into a patera held in the other, and then visiting two cities to be founded one on each side.* Peonius therefore is to be placed toward the end of the two hundred years above mentioned; but it is not exactly known when that term commenced or expired.

The artist, who made the statue, flourished in the ninety fifth Olympiad,† or about one hundred

---

* See Strab. p. 610. In Vitruvius the name of the architect who made this proposal to Alexander is Dinocrates.

In astero aigmi (templum Jovis Olympii Athenis) non uoulo vulgo, sed etiam in paucis a magnificentia nominatur. Nam quemiam locis sunt aedium ornatorum maximorum operibus ornate dispositione, a quibus proprie de his nominationes ehrissimae fama nominantur. Quorum excellentiae, perdoctaeque cogitationum apparentes suspectu habent in Deorum sensitionibus. Primumque aedes Ephesi Dianae Ionico genere ab Ctersiphonte Cnosio et filio ejus Metagene est instituta, quam postea Demetrius ipsius Dianae servus, et Peonius Ephesius dicuntur perfecisse. Mileti Apollinis item Ionicis symmetriis idem Peonius Daphnisque Milesius instituerunt. Eleusine Cereris et Proserpinae.—In Avi, vero Joven Olympium. Vitruv. Praef. L. vii.

Dipteros autem octostylos et pronao et postico, sed circa aedem duplices habet ordines columnarum, uti est aedes Quirini Dorica, et Ephesiae Dianae Ionica a Chersiphonte constituta. L. iii.

Magnificentiae vero admirandae exstat templum Ephesiae Dianae, 200 annis factum a tota Asia.—Operi præfuit Chersiphron Architectus. Plin. L. xxxvi. c. 14, p. 740. Laudatus est et Ctesiphon Gnossius ædis Ephesiæ Dianae admirabili fabricata. L. vii. p. 393.

The manuscripts have, in the above passages, Cresiphon, or Chrysippon, or Chersiphron. The Greek Codices of Strabo seem to have retained the true reading, Chersiphron. Philander.

Jam tum (sub Servio rege) inclutum Dianae Ephesinam; id communiter a civitatibus Asiae factam fama ferebat. Liv. I. c. 15.

Κρηπίς δ' ἐξῆς οικοδομεῖτο τῷ Ἱερῷ, ἥν τε ξέν, ἀιξζηστα ταῦτα καταβαλε αἱ πόλεις. Herodot. L. i. c. 92.

† Nonagesima quinta Olympiade floruere—Canachos—Centoclosus quartodecimo Lysippus fuit, cum et Alexander Magnus.—Ita distinctis celeberrimorum ætatibus, insignes mpho traescorum, reliqua multitudine passim discursa.—Canachos, Apollinem nudum, qui Philesius cognominatur in Didymaeis, Ægineticae aeris temperatura. Cervumque una ita vestigiis suscendit, ut funus subter pedes trahatur, alterna morsu digitis coloque retinentibus solum, ita vertebrato dente utriusque in partibus, ut a repulsu pro vices resiliat. Idem et Celetizontas pueros fecit. Plin. Hist. Nat. L. xxxv. p. 649, 650. Edit. Delph.

Alteralis victim, cum digitis tum calvum credas loetere solo; dexter ita vasti verteberi invelum utrolibet, mobilique ac flexilis in utringue partibus, nec dextra sive sinistra, ut so mensu pellus status alii per vices, hoc est, a looco pellis, dextri; a dextrae, levi resilient. Interpres in loc.

DIDYME.

and twenty-four years after Xerxes destroyed the temple, twenty-two before Alexander's expedition, and three hundred and fifty-six before the Christian æra.

This very eminent master was a Sicyonian, named Canachus, and a scholar of Polycletus, the Argive.* Several of his works are on record, as the boys riding a single horse; — one of the images representing the worthies, who with Lysander acquired renown at Ægospotamos, in the Delphic temple; ‡ the statue of Bucellus, the first Sicyonian who conquered as a pugil among the boys, at Olympia; § and a statue of Venus, at Sicyon, in gold and ivory. He worked in marble also,* as well as in these precious materials; and had a brother, named Aristocles, who was little inferior to him in reputation. ‖

The Apollo Didymæus, or Philesius, as he is sometimes styled, was founded in brass of Æginetic temperature, naked, ⁋ and, as represented on medals of Augustus and Caligula, holding a lyre. By him was a stag ingeniously balanced and contrived, ‡‡ which on a medal of Balbinus he bears in one hand, with his temple in the other. The Apollo Ismenius at Thebes was executed by the same Canochus, in cedar, and resembled this at Didyme so much, that Pausanias remarks, it was easy for one who had seen either, and heard the name of the master, to pronounce by whom the other was made. ‖‖

With what magnificence and prodigious spirit this new edifice was designed, may in some measure be collected from the present remains. Strabo has termed it " the greatest of all temples," adding, it continued without a roof on account of its bigness; Pausanias mentions it as unfinished, but as one of the wonders peculiar to Ionia; and Vitruvius numbers this among the four temples which had raised their architects to the summit of renown.

It is remarkable, the vicinity of a spring was deemed a necessary adjunct to the oracular seats of Apollo, and when those failed, he was supposed to forsake these. Hence their mutual coexistence is insisted on in a response,** given by the god concerning the silent Oracles, in which he declares that innumerable divine oracular sources had burst forth on the surface of the earth, both fountains and whirly exhalations; and some the earth opening had again received into its bosom, and some in a long series of years had perished; but that Apollo still enjoyed the inspiring Mycalesian water in the recess of Didyme, with the Delphic, and that at Clares. ***

Of the three springs which remained, as asserted above, the unabsorbed property of the god, the Castalian has been so much celebrated, that its extraordinary qualities are very generally known. The Clarian seems to have rivalled it in the claim of poetic energy, though less liberal in the communication, the priest only partaking of it. This personage was usually unlearned, and ignorant of metre; yet after hearing solely the number and names of the consulters, going down into the cavern, and drinking of this hidden fountain, he uttered answers composed in verse upon the subjects mentally required by each. He was taken from certain families only, and mostly of Milesus.

From the usages before described, as introductory to the act of prophecy at Branchidæ, it appears that water was sometimes applied there in a different manner, though for obtaining the same end; and, if the prophet did not drink, yet the divine enthusiasm was supposed to be derived from this Mycalean fountain, as it is called, being fabled perhaps to have its source on Mount Mycale, as a water was by the Port Panormus,* against Branchidæ, which, they affirmed, emerged there, after passing, like the Alpheus, through the intermediate sea: for Callisthenes, the historian,† after relating that the prophet of Jupiter Hammon, contrary to the usual mode, had answered Alexander in words, that he was the son of Jupiter, asserted, that the Oracle at Branchidæ having been forsaken by Apollo, and the fountain dried up, from the time Xerxes pillaged the temple, the latter had then flowed anew, and the Milesian ambassadors going to Memphis reported many prophecies concerning the divine birth of Alexander, his future victory at Arbela, the death of Darius, and other great events to come.

The judicious Strabo marks this narration as extravagant; and indeed it may be asked why the Milesians, if their Oracle was then thus prescient, were either so inattentive to it, so irreligious, or ill advised, as to exclude this Alexander,‡ even though admitted by the other Ionian cities, until his gallies arriving, and the Macedonians preparing to storm, they endeavoured to escape, some in skiffs, some on their bucklers, to the island once before the city, as seen in Plate I. but were intercepted at the mouth of the port; about three hundred only getting to it. Alexander, to reduce these, sent vessels provided with ladders to enable the soldiers to ascend the shore, then steep; but on observing they were ready to undergo any extremity, he pardoned them for their bravery, and received them into his service.§

The Branchidæ, who fled with Xerxes, had been permitted to settle among the Bactri, in a region remote from Greece and the dread of punishment. They encompassed their town with walls, and called it by their own name. Alexander, surmounting every obstacle in his way with a rapidity next to incredible, arrived here in five years* after the taking Miletus. Their posterity still retained the primitive manners, but were become double-tongued, not speaking either the language of their progenitors, or that of the country in which they now lived, with purity. They received the king joyfully, surrendering their persons and city. But Alexander, knowing the old grudge, commanded the Milesians who served in his army to be assembled, and referred to them the consideration, which should preponderate, whether the memory of the ancient injury done by the Branchidæ, or a regard for their original extraction. They varied in opinion, and it was signified that he would determine. The following day deputies attended on him from the Branchidæ. He ordered, they should accompany him; and entering the gate with a light-armed party, directed the phalanx to surround the walls, and, on a signal being given, to pillage this receptacle of traitors, putting all to the sword; which they did, unresisted, regardless of the conformity in language, of intreaty, or supplication; and demolished the consecrated groves, dug up the foundations, and erased even the vestiges of the town, so that the site remained a bare solitude and barren waste.† The warmest advocates for Alexander have censured this severity as misplaced, falling not on the real transgressors, but their guiltless descendants, who had never seen Miletus, much less betrayed the temple to Xerxes.‡

As to the silence of the Oracle when deserted by the Branchidæ, it probably continued only until the damage then sustained was so far repaired, as to enable new managers to resume the craft. And this had been accomplished before Alexander got possession of Miletus; for then a Macedonian soldier, named Seleucus,§ who proved afterwards one of his successors, curious of futurity, was said to have consulted concerning his return, and to have received for answer,

Μη σπευδε Ευρωπην, Ασιη τοι πολλον αμεινων.
Haste not to Europe, Asia is far better for you.

And on asking about his death,

Αργος αλευαμενος, το πεπρωμενον ες ετος ιξεις.
Ει δ᾽ Αργος ελασσαι, τοτ᾽ αν ποτμον αυτος εφοιτα.
Avoiding Argos, you will attain your destined age; but if you go to Argos, you may perish by a violent death.

The latter reply made him solicitous in his enquiries after places so called, and cautious not to approach them; the former seeming verified by the exalted station he enjoyed in Asia, as it was finally confirmed by his death, for passing over into Europe in the seventy-third year of his age, and the forty-second of his reign, he was killed at Lysimachia. One instance of the piety for

---

* Arr. Exp. 28. Imperf. 2. Arr. Ch. 528.   ‡ Plutarch, p. 557.   T. & Vol. Paris.
† Q. Curt. l. vii. c. 5. Ælian. Fragm. p. 790. Edit. Hesb, and Suidas in Βραγχιδαι.   § Appian. Syriac. p. 198, 207, 206. Edit. 1670.

which he is celebrated, and of his regard for the temple at Branchidæ, was this, that he restored to it a brazen image of the god, which in the time of Xerxes had been carried away to Ecbatana in Media.*

The two kings and brothers, Seleucus and Antiochus, displayed a like disposition in their veneration for this deity, and munificence to his temple, as appears from a curious record copied by Consul Sherard, who visited this spot in 1709, and again in 1716, published by Chishull.† It was inscribed on a square piece of marble, beneath a shed, on the north side of the temple; and is an epistle of King Seleucus to the Milesians, with a catalogue of the royal donations which accompanied it; the cups, bowls, and utensils, of various sizes and denominations, of gold and silver, exceeding in value one thousand three hundred and fifty pounds sterling; besides precious incense and costly ointments, of which no estimate can be made, and the dedication of twelve altars, with a thousand victims for sacrifice: the occasion being the unexpected safety of Seleucus when supposed to be killed in battle, together with a peace for ten years, agreed on between them and Ptolemy Energetes.‡ Demodamas also, their general, after penetrating beyond the borders of the Sogdiani, where Alexander had founded a third city called by his name, and altars were placed by Bacchus, Hercules, Semiramis, and Cyrus, as memorials of the extent of their expeditions, remembered, thus afar off, the favourite deity of his masters, and on the mutual boundary of the Persian and Scythian territories, erected his altars to Apollo Didymæus.§

Among the benefactors mentioned in another inscription, is Prusias the Third, surnamed Cynegus, or *the Hunter*, King of Bithynia, who dedicated‖ certain first-fruits, probably of the Attalic spoils, as the learned Chishull conjectures: the royal pillager, who had carried off Æsculapius on his own shoulders when he sacked Pergamus, hoping, it is likely, to compensate for his impieties there by his liberality here. The share which this Apollo was reputed to have had in his prosperity, with the veneration shown by his successor for so propitious a deity, is commemorated in verses addressed to his son Nicomedes by Scymnus the Chian. ¶

Such were the offerings of ancient art, with which this temple also, according to Strabo,** was most sumptuously adorned.

From these specimens it may be concluded, the additions made to the sacred repositories, contained, with the Oracle, in distinct cells,†† were inscribed annually on marble; and the curious will regret that so authentic a register, though committed to so durable a substance, has yet not escaped to us entire and legible. It was hoped, the remnants already published might have been enlarged by farther transcripts; but after diligent search among the ruins and rubbish which cover the spot to a considerable extent, some fragments only, too imperfect to be inserted here, were found, excepting the short inscription in the head-piece to this chapter, the single word ΜΝΗΜΗΣ, and the following, in large and plain characters, on a square piece of veined marble, fixed on its side in the wall of a ruined mosque by the temple. It was copied before by Mr. Wood, as well as the two given from Priene and Teos; and by Consul Sherard, being mentioned by Chishull,* as reserved for the second part of his Asiatic Antiquities.

```
ΠΡΟΦΗΤΗΣΑΜΑΚΑΙΣ**
ΥΑΡΧΗΕΜΑΡΚΟΤΟΤΑΠΙΟΥ
ΣΙΑΝΟΥΔΑΜΑΤΟΣΚΥΡΕΙΝ
ΜΙΑΝΟΣΦΙΑΣΑΣΛΑΒΩΝΠΑΡΑ
ΤΗΣΠΑΤΡΙΔΟΣΤΗΝΠΡΟΦΗΥΕ
ΑΝΑΚΑΗΡΩΤΕΙΣΤΟΝΩΝΣΙΚ**ΣΙΥ
ΩΣΙΣΕΦΑΝΗΦΟΡΟΣΓΥΜΝΑΣΙΑΡΧΟ*
ΠΑΤΕΡΩΝΓΕΝΟΥΣΝΑΤΑΡΧΩΝΚΑΙΚΙ
ΤΩΝΗΑΤΡΟΣΦΑΔΑΜΑΜΗΓΡΟΣΔΕΦΑ
ΣΙΑΝΗΣΓΑΑΦΥΡΑΣΑΡΧΙΕΡΕΩΝΤΩΝΣΣ
ΒΑΣΤΩΝΠΟΙΗΣΑΝΤΩΝΘΕΩΡΙΑΣΕΠΙΕ
ΜΕΡΑΣΔΕΚΑΚΑΙΜΟΝΟΜΑΧΙΑΣΑΠΟΤΙ
ΜΟΥΣΠΙΗΜΕΡΑΣΔΕΚΑΔΤΟΚΑΙΑΡΧΙΕΡ
ΩΝΤΗΣΙΩΝΙΑΣΠΟΙΗΣΑΝΤΩΝΔΕΚΑΙΣ
***ΣΕΙΣΚΑΙΔΗΜΟΘΟΙΝΙΑΣΚΑΙΓΥΜΝ
ΑΟΣΕΙ†
```

To the inscriptions discovered here, we owe, among other curious particulars, the knowledge we have of some of the principal officers concerned in the management of the temple. Of these the *Stephanephorus* was the chief priest, so named from his wearing a crown when employed in his function.‡ The prophet reported the answers of the Oracle,§ and was elected by the lots, (a mode of divination, which it is believed the priests could bias or interpret at will) except when superior merit or interest prevented a competition, as in the instance of Flavianus Phileas in the preceding inscription, and of one Posidonius in another, well cut in large characters, on a marble in the wall of a ruined building by a Turkish burying-ground near Miletus, he being chosen by the god, after the lots had thrice made him the *Stephanephorus*.

```
ΕΥΣΕΒΕΣΙΝΚΛΗΡΟΙΕΠΟΕΕΙΣΩΝΙΣ
        ΤΡΙΣΣΕΔΑΚΟΝΤΑ
Δ**ΚΩΜΑΙΣΝΔΙΔΥΜΟΙΣΣΤΕΜ
        ΜΑΣΙΝΑΘΑΝΑΤΟΙΣ
ΤΟΙΩΝΩΝΑΠΟΛΑΩΝΣΠΡΟΦΗΤΩΝ
        ΗΣΠΑΣΑΤΑΥΤΟΣ
ΑΜΜΜΑΚΡΙΣΙΝΜΗΤΡΟΣΤΕΤΕΕΙΗΝ
              ΔΙΚΑΣΑΣ
ΟΥΚΑΓΟΣΟΤΔΑΙΩΝΕΠΙΑΜΕΕΤΑΣ
         ΑΝΔΡΑΓΑΡΣΙΔΕΝ
*ΩΝΠΡΙΝΑΕΙΤΟΥΡΓΩΝΟΤΔΣΝΙΔΡΙ
             ΠΟΜΕΝΟΝ*
```

The præfects and adsessors were entrusted with the custody of the sacred treasures, and the care of the temple and its sanctuary, which required their presence almost continually; and here, the latter met and determined questions of right, probably concerning the privilege of sacrificing and consulting before others, an article of some importance occurring frequently in inscriptions among the favours and honours conferred on particular occasions, as a reward of distinguished merit; and from this power they are termed the *Paredri* or adsessors of Apollo. That such was the nature of this office appears from the account preserved by Strabo † of the Amphictyonic College at Delphi. The number of the præfects and adsessors commonly recorded in the preamble to the inscriptions is two; but in a single instance one only is mentioned, which may have been owing to the death of his colleague; and in another the præfects alone are commemorated with the *Stephanephorus*, and in number six.

Besides these, the poet, and some other officers, of whom we have only very imperfect information, many persons of inferior rank were constantly employed in the service of the temple. The *Hydrophorus*, or water-carrier, was named in a fragment we copied. All these, with the sellers of provision, incense, and other articles necessary to life, or requisite in the heathen worship, settling with their families on the spot, formed a village, within the peribolus of the temple, ‡ supported by the concourse of votaries, and enriched as it were by the immediate influence of the deity; and, as belonging to the god, both accounted and called sacred, § with the district round about it; which for that reason was, on the treaty between the Romans and Antiochus restored by the ten legates to the Milesians, by whom it had been abandoned. ‖

Under the Romans, the arts of prophecy in general, and the Oracles, declined in reputation; that people attending chiefly to the Sibylline books, and the Etruscan modes of divination by entrails, birds, and signs in the air.* To this contemptuous neglect may be partly attributed a chasm in the history of this temple until the reign of Tiberius, when the grand cause of the numerous Greek Asyla, of which many, it was alleged, were arbitrarily established, filling the temples with profligate fugitives of every kind, and producing sedition among the people, by whom their villainies were protected as a matter of religion, was pleaded before the Roman Senate + by deputies from each city, and those from Miletus insisted on a grant from King Darius. The regulations enacted for limiting these sanctuaries were ordered to be engraven on brass, and suspended for a memorial in the temples.

In the year after this transaction, the Asiatic cities decreed a temple to be consecrated at their expense to the Emperor Tiberius, his mother, and the senate, and obtained permission to erect it, for which Nero publicly thanked the fathers and his grandsire.‡ Eleven cities became competitors for the honour of possessing this intended fabric, and Tiberius, with the senate, attended for many days to the allegations of their several ambassadors; after which Smyrna was selected, § it being urged that Pergamus was already distinguished by the temple of Augustus, and Miletus with Ephesus employed on the ceremonies of their respective deities Diana and Apollo.

Absurd and impious as this concession was from Tiberius, it appears modest and rational when compared with the self-deifications of the monster Caligula, who wantonly assumed, or laid aside, the style and character of this or that divinity as caprice suggested; was now a new Bacchus, and presently metamorphosed into an Apollo, his hair encircled with a radiated crown, the bow and arrow in his left hand, and the Graces in his right.¶ He even meditated to rob the deity of his temple at Branchidæ, commanding the Milesians to allot a sacred portion as his own divinity, ** preferring their city, as he pretended, because Ephesus was preoccupied by Diana, Pergamus by Augustus, and Smyrna by Tiberius, but in reality from a design to substitute himself in the room of their Apollo, and to appropriate to his own worship this great and most beautiful fabric,++ which he intended to render more worthy of this distinction by completing what remained unfinished in the structure.‡‡

The attention bestowed on the new and fashionable divinities, many self-created, about this time, diminished the popular esteem and veneration before possessed by the old set, already languishing with age, and gradually tending to decay. Hence at Branchidæ an altar was shown made

* Strabo, p. 814.
+ Ann. 4 b. 22. l. C. 77 a. Tacit. Annal. l. iii. c. 60, 63.
‡ Tacit. l. iv. c. 15. Ann. l. C. 776. Ch. 23.
§ Ann. l. C. 779. Ch. 26. Tacit. l. iv. c. 55, 56.
‖ Tacit. Ann. l. iv. c. 37.
¶ Philo Jud. p. 580. Edit. 1742.
** Zonaras, p. 539.

†† Dion. Cassius, p. 833. Edit. 1742.
‡‡ Milesii Didymæum peregere. Sueton. Vit. Caligul. 21. In other authors also this edifice is sometimes styled the Didymæum.
This circumstance probably is alluded to on a medal of Caligula, on which is a naked Apollo holding the lyre, with the legend MIΛHΣIΩN ΔIΔYMEYΣ. V. Chish. p. 90.

by Hercules the Theban, as the Milesians affirmed, with the blood of victims;[+] but Pausanias, who relates this article, adds, that latterly the blood of the sacrifices had not arisen to any amazing bulk. And the Oracles, which had been artfully founded on reigning superstition by an industrious and crafty priesthood, necessarily declined in reputation with the deity to whom each belonged, but still continued to linger on, revered by the devotee and derided by the philosopher, until their final period, which happened sooner or later in proportion to the abilities of their respective managers; now affording matter of just wonder that such contemptible frauds could subsist so long on human credulity.

From the specimens produced in the preceding pages, the reader will have conceived but a mean idea of the oracular responses uttered at Branchidæ, which, as in other places, were commonly enigmatical, equivocal, ambiguous and unsatisfactory, as will be farther evinced in the sequel of this narration, as well as by the two following instances, which may serve also for examples of the versification, from which the Oracle derived some renown.[‡]

It happened that nine woodcutters were found dead on the mountains. The neighbouring peasants consulted Apollo on this occasion, who replied, these were struck dead by Pan, that Diana had interposed to rescue the others, and that it behoved them to render her propitious by supplication.[§]

Another question proposed was, whether it was proper to take an oath when required. The reply contained a recital of the manner in which the deities were engaged by their pleasures or occupations,[‖] totally evasive, unless it be construed to imply that they had no regard to this matter.

The god, however, ventured sometimes to answer explicitly, when the question had no dangerous tendency, and he was certain never to be contradicted. Thus, when consulted concerning the soul, whether it was immortal, he replied expressly in the affirmative.[¶]

---

* Pausan. L. v. p. 410.
+ At Delos, Apollo had on other occasions offered with the horns, and in Herodes one composed of the ashes of his victims. Potter, p. 283, 290.
‡ Liv. I. xxxviii. c. 12.

This position is said to have been first maintained and spread among the heathens by Thales, a native of Miletus.

The futility of the responses in general supposed to be dictated by Apollo Didymæus, if we may judge from those extant, with his impotency in avenging the insult of Aristodicus, and in protecting his own property from the Branchidæ and Xerxes, to omit any farther instances, was so great, we may reasonably wonder that it did not destroy in an early age the reputation of the god and Oracle, and still more, that both continued in some esteem long after paganism itself began to decline.

Lucian, who lived under the Antonines, relates, that a priest of Tyana consulted the pseudo-prophet Alexander. Whether the Oracles then delivered at Didyme, Claros, and Delphi, were really given by Apollo; but was answered, that was a secret not proper for him to know: and, that the impostor endeavoured to procure the good will of the Didymæan Oracle by frequently recommending it to his followers, saying,*

> Βαϊζοιτων εἰϛ τοὺϛ τοῦ διδυμέος, καὶ ἀκουετε χρησμων.
> Go to the temple of the Branchidæ, and listen to the Oracles.

Another author, who flourished about the time of the emperor Severus, Clemens of Alexandria, after degrading the gentile temples, though lofty, magnificent, and sumptuously adorned, as sometimes places of burial, and receptacles of dead carcases, instances, with Arnobius, this at Branchidæ among others, a Milesian writer relating that Clearchus was interred in it.†

At what period the Clarian Oracle finally ceased is not certainly known. It was extinct when Strabo wrote,‡ but revived again, was consulted by Germanicus,§ and foretold, obscurely, his untimely death. It is mentioned also by Lucian as still existing, with the Delphic and Didymæan; and afterwards by Iamblichus, who lived about the age of Constantine. This emperor removed the sacred tripods from Delphi to Constantinople, and fixed them in the Hippodrome, adorning his city with the statues of the heathen gods and the pillage of their temples. And the Delphic Oracle soon afterwards declined being consulted, bidding his messengers acquaint Julian that the temple was prostrate on the ground, and Apollo no longer possessed his prophetic laurel, or speaking fountain, but that even the beautiful water was extinct.

The fortune, which the Didymæan temple experienced under Constantine, is not perhaps on record; but the Oracle, which survived that crisis so extensively fatal to gentilism, was consulted by Licinius, his colleague in the empire, concerning the event of the war they were about to

---

* Lucian. Alexʰ. vel Ps. T. 2. p. 239. Edit. 1743.
† Clemens Alexand. p. 39. Edit. Oxon. Arnob. adv. Gentes, l. vi. p. 195. Diog. Laert. l. i.
‡ Strabo, p. 642.

§ Ann. l. ii. C. 22, 23. Ch. 18. Tacit. Annal. l. ii. c. 54.
∥ Βαϊζετ᾽ εις Βραγχιδ᾽, χρησμων επαΐσθαι ἁγνων.
  Clem. Cohort. ad gentiles, καὶ μαντειαι ληρωσιν.
  Οὐ παροϛ ἀνδρασιν, ητοι θνητοιϛ ἀσπειθεα θυμῳ. Theodore.

commence with each other: and, it was affirmed, the dæmon replied in a couplet from Homer,* being part of Diomed's speech to Nestor, when surrounded with enemies, and in imminent danger from Hector. "Youthful warriors assail thee, thy vigour is gone, and grievous old age comes upon thee:" and this answer was supposed to be verified, Constantine prevailing, and his competitor being reduced to live privately at Thessalonica, where he was afterwards killed.

In the mutual struggles which ensued between Gentilism and Christianity, it is likely, that Apollo Didymæus was exalted by one party, and depreciated by the other, and his temple honoured or neglected in proportion as either prevailed most in its neighbourhood, until the apostacy of Julian; an æra, when his worship reflourished, and the god arose again in glory with an emperor for his prophet.

This great restorer and reformer of the Greek ritual distinguished the Didymæan temple with evident marks of his superior regard. The Christians having erected oratories near to it in honour of their martyrs, he wrote to the governor of Caria+ to consume them with fire if they had a roof and the sacred table; and, even if unfinished, to dig up the very foundations. He added to the dignity of the prophetical office by accepting it, and to the authority of the Oracles by citing them with encomiums, as at first admonitory, and still didactic: which he exemplified in lines,‡ confirming his injunction for paying due reverence, as to the magistrate, so also to the priest. Moreover, when filled with consternation by fatal presages from the victims offered to Mars on a victory over the Persians, he consulted this Apollo concerning the future event of the war. He was deluded by the reply, which declared that Jupiter had overcome the giants and Julian his enemies. § He engaged the Persians, and was killed by an unknown hand; ‖ his army was preyed on by famine, and a dishonourable peace concluded.

About this time it is likely the Carians asked, whether they should admit the Milesians into their alliance against the Persians, and were answered by the Oracle.¶

Πάλαι ποτ᾽ ἦσαν ἄλκιμοι Μιλήσιοι.
The Milesians once were brave.

It is related, that in the battle which ensued, the Milesians were all slain.*

Thus far may be traced from ancient materials the various fortunes of the Didymæan Apollo. At what period the holy treasure of this temple was pillaged, whether under Nero,† when Acratus and Secundus Carinates were commissioned to plunder Asia and Achaia, and carried away the votive offerings and sacred images; or, at the reformation under Constantine and the first christian emperors, when the silver or golden ornaments and utensils of the temples in general were melted down and confiscated, with the statues, except the brazen which were removed from all sides to Constantinople; or, at what other crisis; and also, when the temple was ruined, and the Oracle became finally silent, is not, it is believed, now on record; neither have we any notices of its fate from the death of Julian to the journey from Smyrna, referred to in the Chapter on Priene, being a term of one thousand three hundred and ten years.

From the very rude draught of part of the front of the temple, published with that account by Wheler, and again by Chishull, it appears, that besides the two columns supporting their architrave, two more remained, of which one, with a pilaster and a portion of the cell then standing, is fallen since. The heap rises less high on the sides, than at the angles, and has in the middle, or within the cell, a large vacant space, which, if the temple had been roofed, would, it is likely, have been also covered. By this, and among the stones, grow several fig and other full-grown trees.

Plain traces of its extensive peribolus are yet seen; but the two admired groves, of which one stood within it, ‡ are now represented only by a few solitary trees, scattered bushes, and thickets of mastic. Some spots between these are cultivated with Turkey and common wheat; and it is observable the soil was anciently noted as fruitful in this grain.§ Among the tall stubble of the former were placed several beehives, being long wooden trunks, headed like a barrel, piled up one on another, belonging, with the produce of the ground, to the few wretched inhabitants of a small place, remote about half an hour, named Ura.

The solicitude, which Julian showed, to re-establish and confirm Apollo in the sole possession of this spot, prolonged only the term of his enjoyment; and the god, probably soon after the death

---

* Another answer of the Milesian Apollo, with remarks on it, may be found in Lactantius, L. iv. c. 13.

He is cited also in Stobæus. Καὶ Θεσπίδας, καὶως ἀπακτον (τινι) δηλοῖ, τῇ Ἑαυτοῦ πηγῇ, οὗτος ἀνηρ εἰς ἔλκε νῶν ἐ'ε ἐνέγκας τοῦ Ἑλληνι ἀπεζη δ τῶν καὶ ὁ Θεὸς χρᾷ διαι τοὺτοις τὸ, Δακεδαιμίος ἠμή, ματ᾽ζωη τὸ στηρηεπετιμηλέλατο, ἵνα λεγε Οτ. ω. κατίθα με, οὐ λεγε, τὴν νόσ, ζ απαι οὖν ἀπο τοιιοτεχωνος χρησος γομή ἀι ταῦτ ωρίσιαμ. Ex Iamblichi Epist. ad Dexippum de Dialectica. Serm. lxxix. p. 471.

† Ann. l. 4. 817. Ch. 61. Tacit. Ann. L. xv. c. 45.

‡ Strab. p. 634.

§ Διδοῖ δ᾽ ἐρίσας δουχμα τελεσφρον αρουρα Ἐσρ.θ.θας, και πιονι γαιειῃ Μιλήτου, Ταῦα μεν αλεψαις παλντεσαν, Μιονδὰ.
Dioscoron Argonaut. v. 150.

This spot furnished also auxiliaries to Priam:
Οἱ Μιλητον εχοντες —
Νασ...ι τ᾽ αιπεια ποσιω, και νηιόν Μυκάλης.
ΠΑΡΑΛΗΠΟΜ. ΟΜΗΡΟΥ. L. i. v. 290.

of his royal prophet and patron, was constrained to yield it up to Christianity; and this again, in process of time, to admit Mahometanism to the larger portion, if not to an exclusive tenure of the whole. Some broken pillars and pieces of wall mark the situation of one or more Greek churches, by which we found the cross cut on two fragments. The ruin of a small ordinary mosque, unroofed, stands near the temple, with part of a flight of steps on the outside, once leading to the minaret; and another was erected upon the large heap seen in the view, near the two columns, a fragment of the wall remaining, with steps also annexed, as in the above, and other Turkish ruins at Miletus, and elsewhere.

The vestiges of the town, besides many wells, consist in low walls and rubbish, spreading to some extent about the temple, with a round building, nearer to the sea, probably intended for a beacon or watch-tower. All these were very mean, though composed, it is likely, of materials supplied by the temple, and broken or made portable by fire: the cavities, over which several of the furnaces were constructed, being visible close by, particularly on the side toward the sea, and before the front. Indeed, it may be conjectured from the prodigious quantity of marble destroyed or consumed, that the lime or cement so procured, was the staple commodity of the place, and that, as the ancient inhabitants were maintained by the prosperity of the temple, the later subsisted for a time on the ruin. However, the vastness of the heap in general, with the many stones of great magnitude, the majesty of the columns yet entire, with the beauty of the numerous capitals and ornamental members thrown down, and as remarkable for the delicacy of their workmanship as for the amazing elegance of their design, is still such, as must impress even the tasteless spectator with reverential regret; and excited, not unworthily, in the journalist of the Tour from Smyrna, to whom its name and history were unknown, a persuasion, that this fabric had certainly been one of the Seven Wonders of the World.

PLATE I.

MAP OF THE COUNTRY AROUND THE TEMPLE.

The temple of Apollo-Didymæus is situated not far distant from the promontory of Posidium. It is about two miles and a half from the nearest shore, and twenty-two miles and a half from Miletus. It is situated in a plain, which slopes gently towards the sea. The port Panormus is still frequented by small vessels, and is protected by a circular pier, of ancient construction, formed of large masses of marble. Around it are the remains of dwellings and buildings, now almost concealed by thickets of myrtle, mastic, and ever-greens.

Nearly mid-way between the temple and the port commences the sacred way, lying in a hollow between two gently sloping banks, along which are placed, at certain intervals, sepulchres and statues of ancient workmanship: between sixty and seventy of these are still visible. All of them bear the manifest indications of the Egyptian school. Most of the statues are sitting figures, upon chairs or seats of a very ancient form; some of these have inscriptions inscribed in the Boustrophedon mode of writing. Amongst them is the statue of a lion, of white marble, with the Egyptian head. Much of the marble used in the construction of the temple resembles the Parian; but there is also a great intermixture of materials of a less pure conformation.

When Chandler visited the temple, there were no habitations nearer than Ura, about two miles distant on the road towards Miletus, now called Palatia; the modern village surrounding the temple having been deserted. It appears to be reviving; and the diminution of the ancient materials is unfortunately the consequence of its encreasing prosperity. In the interval of a few months which occurred between the two visits made by the gentlemen of the mission, a manifest dilapidation had taken place. Part of the wall of the pronaos had been destroyed, and a beautiful terebinth tree, the boast of the village, cut down. A windmill usurped the place of this sacred object; in the construction of which many of the less massive blocks, particularly those enriched with sculpture, were employed, and some converted into cement used in building it. The two Corinthian capitals were totally destroyed, and some of the statues had been grievously defaced. The evil was unfortunately progressive; and nothing appeared likely to check the gradual, yet certain destruction of the temple, but one of those visitations, which in Asia Minor sometimes depopulates a whole country, and converts the busy haunt of man to a solitary waste.

The temple appears to have been thrown down by an earthquake, another of those awful visitations which compel mankind to abandon their dwellings, and seek a more secure residence at a distance from their former abodes.

The modern village, now called Jeronta, consists of about an hundred and fifty houses. The whole of the tract abounds with marble fragments and remains of ancient inscriptions.

PLATE II.

VIEW OF THE TEMPLE OF APOLLO DIDYMÆUS.

PLATE III.

PLAN OF THE TEMPLE.

The plan of the temple is a parallelogram, three hundred and three feet six inches in length, by one hundred and sixty-four feet five inches in width, measured upon the upper step. The cella is surrounded by a double row of columns, the outer peristyle having twenty-one columns in the sides, and ten in each front.

The walls within the cella are divided into compartments by pilasters placed at equal distances all around, excepting at the entrances, where there are two semi-columns of the Corinthian order. This mode of ornamenting the interior of the cella is uncommon in the temples of Greece, but prevails in the temples of Rome, as well as in those of Balbec and Palmyra.

There was only one entrance to the temple through the pronaos at the east end, which was of considerable depth, and separated from the cella by another division of about twenty-six feet; the use of which is difficult to be imagined, unless it may be considered as the treasury of the temple, where the donaria were exposed to the view of the people; access to them being defended by bars of metal. The opisthodomus of the Parthenon of Athens was a division of similar construction, and planned for a similar purpose.

The wall of the cella in the back front is eight feet ten inches in thickness; it is solid, and faced within and without with large blocks of marble, of a colour inclining to grey: they are left rough and unpolished. The interior of the walls is composed of the common stone of the country.

When Mr. Wood visited this temple, he found two Turkish masons employed in carrying off all the portable marbles for tombstones; he is of opinion, that the very extraordinary and confused manner in which the massy stones of this edifice are piled over the remains of the walls, must have resulted from the effects of a violent earthquake; the walls not being overthrown, but in a manner crushed down, and the remnants concealed under the mass, which extends equally on both sides.

Many of the stones lying on the north side of the temple are inscribed with one, two, or more letters; several with ΣΟΣΟ and ΜΟΕΝ. They formed part of the cella walls, and the characters were on the external face.

The columns of the inner peristyle are fluted the whole length of their shafts; but those of the external range only to a distance of two feet below the capitals, the rest of their shafts being left rough, excepting a few inches above the apophyges, which, as this temple was never completed, evidently proves that the flutings were finished after the columns were raised.

The columns were put together with all possible precaution, to insure their stability. In the upper surface of one of the frusta, part of an angular column, there are no less than twelve holes, worked to receive cramps of metal; besides that for the plug in the centre, which was eighteen inches in diameter. The holes for the cramps are symmetrically disposed over the bed or surface,

PLATE IV.

ELEVATION OF THE FRONT OF THE TEMPLE.

The reader is here presented with the front of this stupendous edifice restored, as far as the authorities accessible on the spot permitted. No part of the cornice could be discovered, nor any circumstances conclusive, as to the inclination of the pediment. The columns are more than nine diameters and a half in height, a very unusual excess in the proportion of columns of Ionic buildings. The great extent of a decastyle front was probably the motive which determined the projector of the edifice to increase the proportion generally observed in the length of the shaft.

It is dangerous to deduce principles from individual examples. The proportions observed in the shafts of the columns, might have led to the inference, that a greater number of columns in the front, whilst it demanded a proportionate reduction in the intervals in order to contract the extent, which would otherwise be too great, seemed to require the elongation of the shaft, as a collateral expedient, to bring the height and width to due proportion. In the present instance this object does not appear to have been contemplated, or it might have been effected, by increasing the depth of the epistylia and zophorus, or frieze, both of which are made considerably less than was customary in the best times of Grecian architecture. The apparent weakness of the epistylia is one of the great defects of this building, and is scarcely to be reconciled to the exquisite finish of all the parts, considering this as amongst the true tests of architectural perfection.

PLATE V.

THE ORDER OF THE COLUMNS.

Fig. 1. The uppermost step, base, and lower part of the shaft of the columns belonging to the outer peristyle.

The step, together with the scotia, astragals, and fillets, are formed out of one block of marble. The torus is worked in the lower frustum of the shaft.

Fig. 2. The capital of the columns, with the upper part of the shaft, and the epistylia.

The hem, or border, in the front of the volutes of the capitals of the exterior peristyle is left square; but that of the internal peristyle is wrought circularly. The flowers resting on the echinus of the former have only three petals, but those of the latter have four.

PLATE VI.

DETAILS OF THE ORDER.

The upper figures represent the flank of the Ionic capitals, with a section made by a plane passing through the centre of the pulvinar, or cushion. Below them the plan of the capitals is shown, with a section made by a plane passing through the centre of the face of the capitals.

The lower figure represents the epistylia of the outer peristyle, together with its internal face, and that of the faire above it

PLATE VII.

THE CAPITALS OF THE ANTÆ.

Several of the capitals belonging to the interior pilasters remain lying on the north side of the temple. The returns are not quite half the width of the front, whence it is evident that none of them belonged to the antæ of the pronaos; for one of the returns in these is always equal in width to the front, corresponding to the width of the epistylia supported by the columns placed intermediately between the terminations of the walls of the cella.

There are also several remains of the ornamental pieces filling the intervals between the capitals of the antæ within the cella, which are represented in the following plate.

The joint between the capital and the antæ takes place immediately below the bead which conceals it.

The capitals are not all similar; the design of the compartment between the horns of the capital varies. A variety is given in the figure at the bottom of the plate.

PLATE VIII.

DETAILS OF THE INTERIOR

The ornamental frize, in which griffins and lyres are introduced, filled the intervals between the capitals of the antæ within the cella. The griffin is usually composed of the head and wings of an eagle; with the body, legs and tail, of a lion. In this frize it has the head of a lion, with the horns and beard of a goat.

As the ancients adorned the statues and temples of their gods with symbols of their supposed influence, the griffin, which was particularly sacred to Apollo, and in fabulous antiquity believed to be ever watching the golden mines on the Scythian and Hyperborean mountains; the griffin is here introduced as guardian of the lyre, which belonged to Apollo, as the inventor of music.

It has a lion's head: because Apollo, or the sun, is most powerful when in that sign of the zodiac. It may be added, the Persians had a statue of him, with the head of this animal. The goat's horns and beard may have been adopted from the goat of metal offered by the Cleonæans at Delphi, as a memorial of their deliverance from a plague, on sacrificing, as they were advised to do, a goat to Apollo, or the sun, at his rising.

The Corinthian capital belongs to the columns engaged in the wall on entering the cella. The volutes were destroyed, but they are supplied from conjecture in the figure which represents half the capital upon a larger scale.

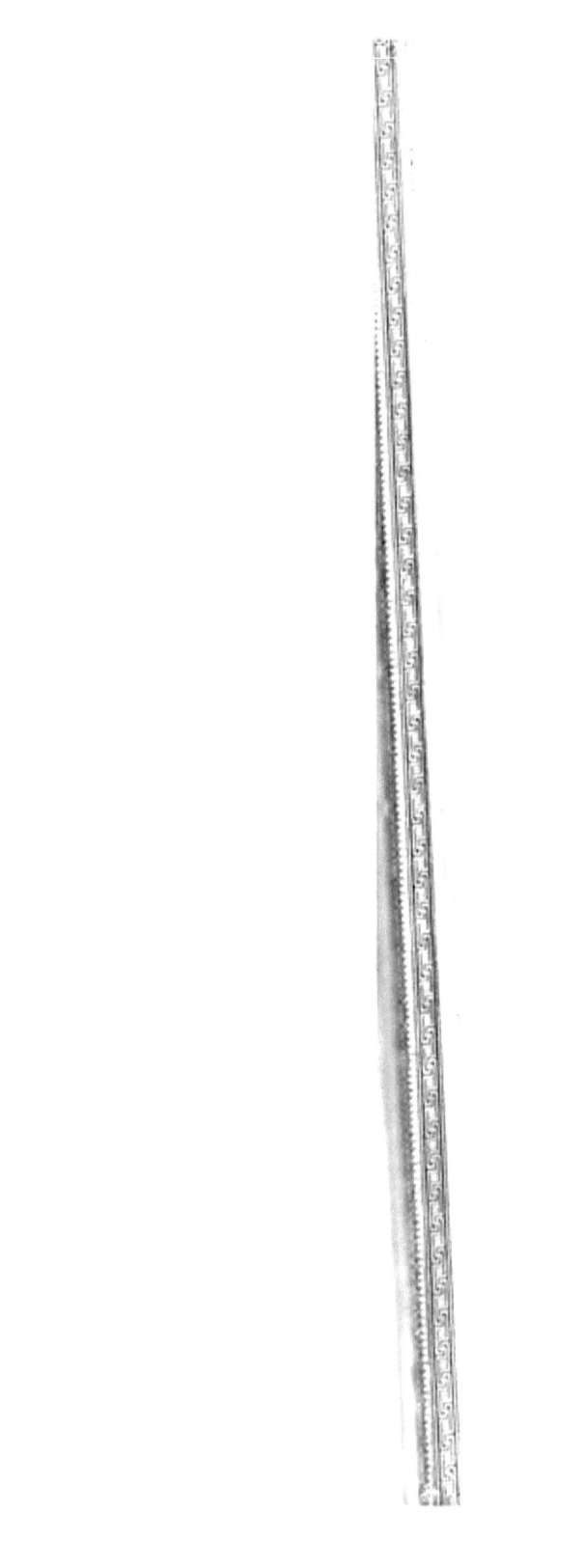

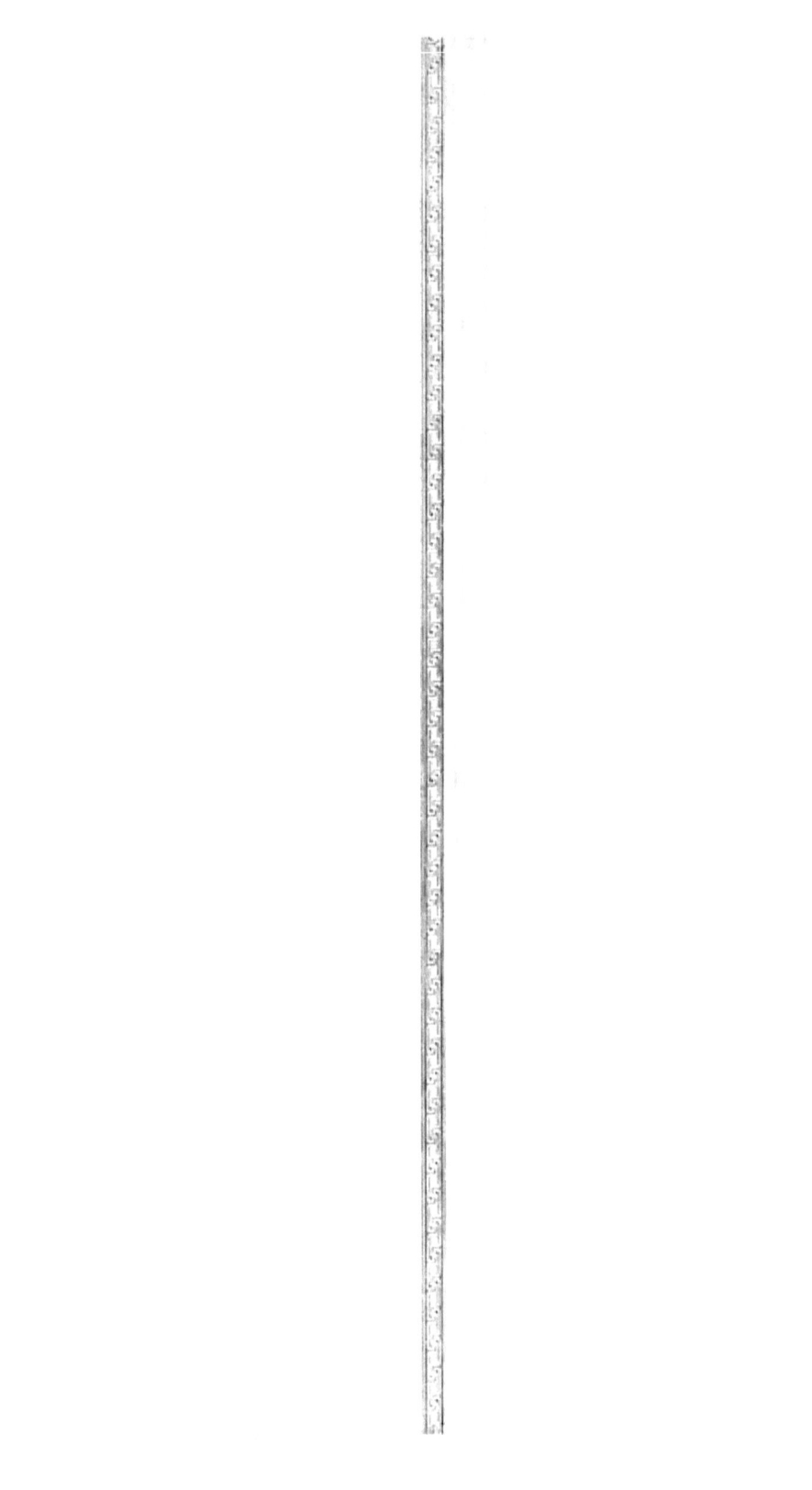

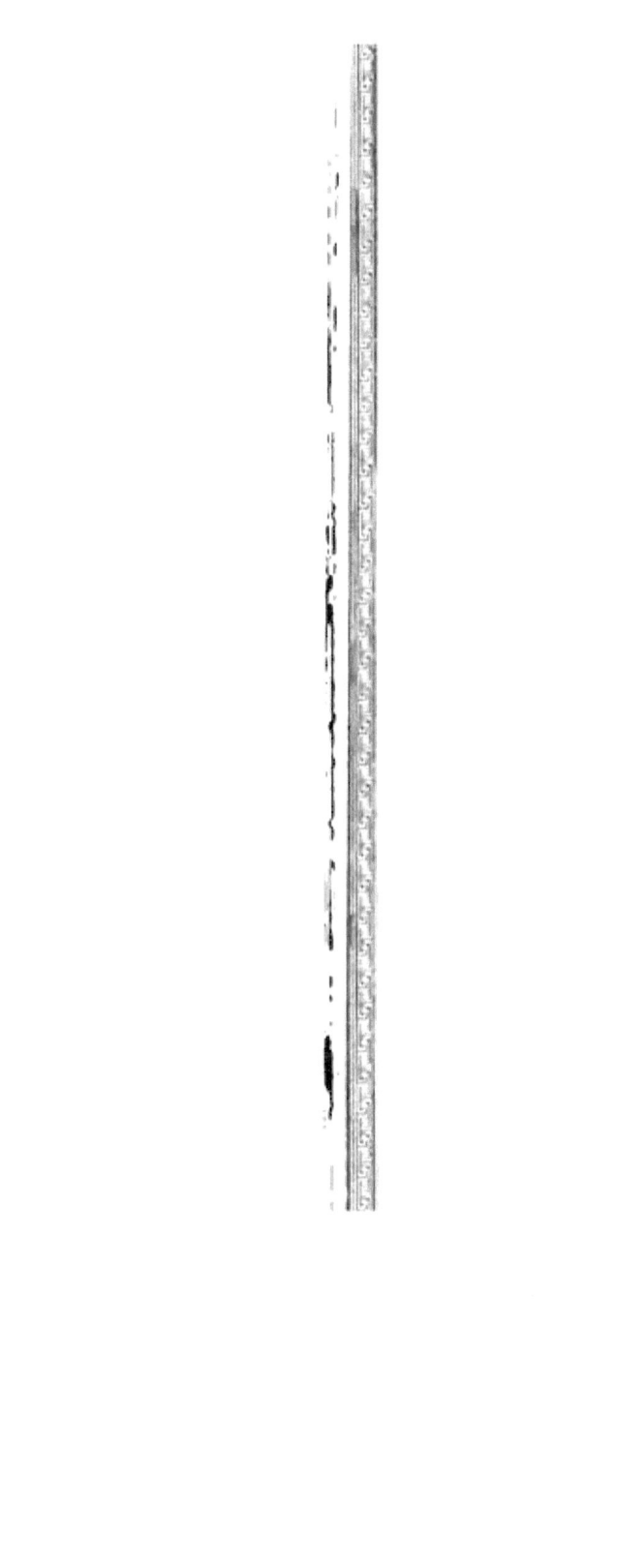

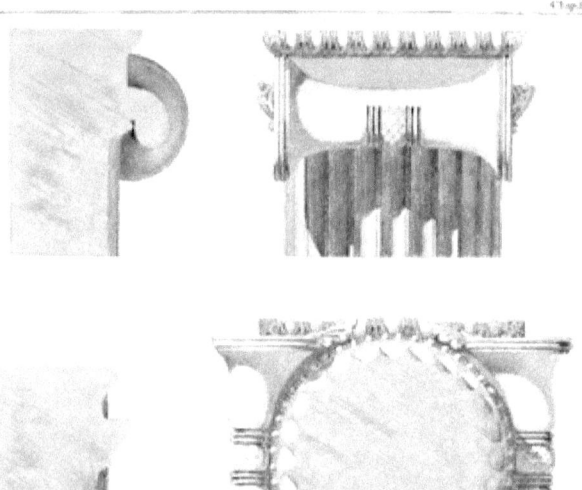
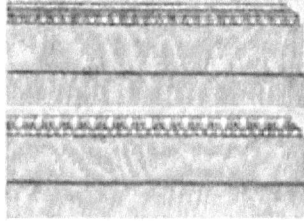

CHAPTER IV.

LABRANDA.

The superb titles of Neokoroi, of Supreme Guardians and Directors of Asia, assumed by the votaries of their tutelar deities with ostentation and triumph, were beheld with a jealous eye by those who, under a different form of religious institution, were yet candidates for a like pre-eminence.

The temple, which is chosen for the subject of the present chapter, cannot boast a proud an origin. Its magnificence, however, the choice and richness of the materials employed, together with the inscriptions, with which the columns were decorated, might, as its founders appear to have imagined, have secured its name and memorial to posterity. The style of the architecture, the form of the inscriptions, the names and titles of the magistrates recorded, may possibly induce us to fix the æra of its construction to the time of the Antonines. The freedom of the Grecian republics would scarcely have allowed their magistrates so distinguished an honour; but the modesty of more ancient times soon gave way to the arbitrary regulations of proconsular government.

Notwithstanding these advantages and helps which antecedent enquiry, it must be confessed that little can be collected relating to the antiquity of this building; for even the name of the district, in which it stands has been differently given by those travellers who have recently and attentively visited the spot, and from whom alone any satisfactory illustration of the subject can be expected. The several authorities are now given, that in a point of so much obscurity, the reader may be furnished with every possible assistance which the nature of the enquiry will admit. The account which Dr. Chandler has given is as follows:

" On the way from Iasus to Mendelet, which is distant four hours, and three from Mylasa, we left the level green; and riding northwards, through stubble of Turkish wheat, came in an hour to a beautiful and extensive plain, covered with vines, olive and fig trees, and flocks and herds feeding; and skirted by mountains, with villages. We crossed it by a winding road, with the country-house of the Aga of Mylasa on our right hand; and passing a village called Jackly, unexpectedly discovered the solemn ruins of a temple; but, as it was dusk, we continued our journey to Meuselet, which was an hour farther on. The temple was of the Corinthian order, sixteen columns, with part of their entablature standing; the cell and roof demolished. It is in a nook, or recess; the front, which is toward the east, close by the mountain-foot; the back and one side overlooking the plain. The style of the architecture is noble, and made us regret that some members, and in particular the angle of the cornice, were wanting. Its marbles have been melted away, as it were piece-meal, in the furnaces for making lime, which are still in use, close by the ruin. A town has ranged with the temple on the north. The wall, beginning near it, makes a circuit on the hill, and descends on the side toward Meuselet. The thickets, which have over-run the site, are almost impenetrable, and prevented my pursuing it to the top; but the lower portion may easily be traced. It had square towers at intervals, and was of a similar construction with the wall at Ephesus. Within it is a theatre cut in the rock, with some seats remaining. In the vineyards beneath, are broken columns, and marble fragments; and in one, behind the temple, two massive sarcophagi, carved with festoons and heads; the lids on, and a hole made by force in their sides. They are raised on a pediment, and, as you approach, appear like two piers of a gateway. Beyond the temple are also some ruins of sepulchres: I was much disappointed in finding no inscriptions to inform us of the name of this deserted place, which, from its position on a mountain by the way-side, and its distance from Mylasa, I am inclined to believe was Labranda.

"Labranda," according to Strabo, was a village seated on a mountain in the road from Alabanda to Mylasa. The temple was ancient, and the image of wood. This was styled the Military Jupiter, and was worshipped by the people all around. The way was paved near sixty stadia, or eight miles and a half, as far as Mylasa, and called sacred from the victims and processions, which passed on it. The priesthood of the temple was conferred on the most illustrious of the citizens, and was an officer held for life.

LABRANDA.

"The ruin of this temple coincides with the description of it given by the geographer. The fabric, tottering with age, was, it seems, after his time, gradually renewed, and chiefly by the contributions of the Stephanephori, or high priests; for on seven of the columns is an inscription, which may be thus translated:

> LEO QUINTUS, SON OF LEO, WHEN STEPHANEPHORUS,
> GAVE THIS COLUMN, AS HE HAD PROMISED,
> WITH THE BASE AND CAPITAL.

and the following inscription is repeated on five or more of the columns, with some variation, as to the length of the lines, and the ligatures of the letters:

> MENECRATES, SON OF MENECRATES, CHIEF PHYSICIAN OF THE CITY, WHEN STEPHANE-
> PHORUS, GAVE THIS COLUMN, WITH THE BASE AND CAPITAL. TRYPHENA HIS
> DAUGHTER, HERSELF LIKEWISE STEPHANEPHORUS AND GYMNASIARCH, HAVING
> PROVIDED IT.

"From the form of certain characters in the later inscriptions, it may be inferred, that Leo was the earlier benefactor."*

(Chandler, Asia, chap. lviii.)

Monsieur de Choiseul, Voyage de la Grèce, chap. xi.

"L'emplacement de la ville de Kiselgick n'offre aucunes ruines; mais à environ une lieue au midi, on trouve celles d'une ville ancienne, parmi lesquelles on distingue les restes d'un théâtre, et la plus grande partie d'un temple magnifique. Nous ne pûmes malheureusement découvrir aucune inscription, qui nous indiquât le nom de cette ville. Chandler, s'appuyant sur la situation de ce temple élevé dans une montagne, et environ à deux heures de chemin de Mylasa, comme l'étoit celui de Jupiter Stratius suivant Strabon et Elien, croit que c'est l'ancien bourg de Labranda; mais il n'auroit pas commis cette erreur, s'il eût bien connu le passage de Strabon, qui dit positivement que ce bourg se trouvoit sur la route de Mylasa à Malanda. Cette dernière ville, très-reculée dans la Carie, étoit au nord-est de Mylasa, comme on peut le voir dans la carte; et Kiselgick se trouve au contraire au nord-ouest; on ne peut raisonnablement supposer que la route ait un détour assez considérable, pour aller passer par un lieu éloigné de 90 degrés de la route directe. Les ruines ne paroissent donc pas appartenir au bourg de Labranda; je croirois plutôt que ce sont celles de la ville d'Euromus, et la chaîne de montagnes qui se termine à cet endroit m'en paroît une preuve.

"Strabon, lib. xiv. en décrivant la position d'Euromus, dit,† qu'une montagne appellée Grius et qu'il ne faut point confondre avec le Latmus, prenant son commencement au territoire de Milet

---

* The Mylasians were the proprietors of the famous Jupiter of Labranda. The god often occurs on medals holding the double hatchet, which was his symbol. (See the vignette to the Introduction.)

† [Greek text illegible]

s'avance vers l'orient dans la Carie, jusqu'à ce qu'elle rencontre Chalcetores et Euromus, et qu'elle finit et reste comme suspendue au-dessus de cette dernière ville.

" L'inspection des lieux ne m'a point permis de révoquer en doute l'opinion que je propose. Cette ville d'Euromus n'a jamais été considérable ; il en est cependant parlé plusieurs fois dans Tite Live,* Polybe, et Pline.† Quant à la ville de Calcetores, je serois assez tenté de croire qu'elle étoit située de l'autre côté de Grius à la place d'un méchant village dans lequel j'ai passé, et qui s'appelle aujourd'hui Tarismanta."

PLATE I.

VIEW OF THE TEMPLE.

The view is taken from a point east of north. The principal front faces the east.

PLATE II.

PLAN OF THE TEMPLE.

The darker shade distinguishes the columns which are entire, and those parts of the walls still standing, to a considerable height. The lighter shade shews those parts of which the bases and substructure remain.

The temple was hexastyle, with eleven columns in the flanks. The intervals are very nearly equal to twice the diameter of the columns.

A A. The peristyle.
B. Pronaos.
C. Cella.
D. Posticum.

The pavement in the pronaos and posticum, as well as the columns of both, have been destroyed ; but it is evident that the pavement of the pronaos was raised a step above that of the portico.

PLATE III.

ELEVATION OF THE ORDER.

Fig. 1. Two of the columns of the temple, shewing the intercolumniation. The columns, excepting those on the south side of the temple, are fluted. They have tablets in the front, on which are inscribed the names of the benefactors at whose expense they were erected and finished. One of the inscriptions engraved upon the columns is as follows :

```
         ΛΕΩΝΑΚΟΝΤΟΣ
         ΚΟΙΝΤΟΣΣΤΕΦΑΝΗ
         ΦΟΡΩΝΕΥΤΝΟΣΧΕΣΙ
         ΩΣΤΟΝΚΕΙΟΝΑΛΤΝ
         ΣΠΕΙΡΗΚΑΙΚΕΦΑΛΗΣ
```

The steps lie concealed under the ruins, and by the accumulation of earth around the building. Part of the uppermost is exposed, but their number could not be ascertained.

Fig. 2. Section through the order, which shews the internal face of the epistylium and frieze.

PLATE IV.

DETAILS OF THE BUILDING.

Fig. 1. Base of the columns, with the uppermost step. The projection in the front of this step has the appearance of an ovolo, but it is so much defaced as to make it doubtful whether intended for such, or only meant to preserve the edge of the step from injury whilst the fabric was raising, and the ornamental parts, which are still unfinished, completed.

Fig. 2. Base of the antæ in the front of the pronaos and posticum. The course, on which the bases of the antæ are placed, projects four inches and a half beyond their plinths, and appears to have been part of the original pavement. The steps in front of the pronaos and posticum were formed by the continued plinth of the columns.

Fig. 3. Base of the antæ continued within the humeri, or lateral walls, of the pronaos.

Fig. 4. The door-jamb, with the step on which it is placed. Its height is twenty feet three inches.

Fig. 5. Lateral face of the door-jamb, with a section through the step.

Fig. 6. Internal face of the door-jamb. The cymatium is defaced : it is formed by a straight line only, instead of an ovolo, and a listel.

Fig. 7. Fragment found within the portico. It was probably a portion of the frize continued around the body of the temple.

PLATE V.

ORDER OF THE COLUMNS.

Fig. 1. The entablature and the capital of the columns. The entablature is left plain; it was probably intended to have been decorated to accompany the columns, which are finished. This circumstance, with that of the columns on the south side of the temple not being fluted, shews, beyond a doubt, that the ancients were accustomed to finish the decorations after the fabric was raised. The temple of Apollo Didymæus furnished another example of this practice.

The sima upon the cornice was too much defaced to admit of its height, or projection, being taken; but the height is here restored, by taking the height of the architrave for the mean between the frize and the cornice, including the sima; it was decorated with lions' heads.

Fig. 2. Section through the capital and architrave, shewing the internal face of the latter, with the pannel in its soffit. The dentils were omitted in the cornice of the pediment.

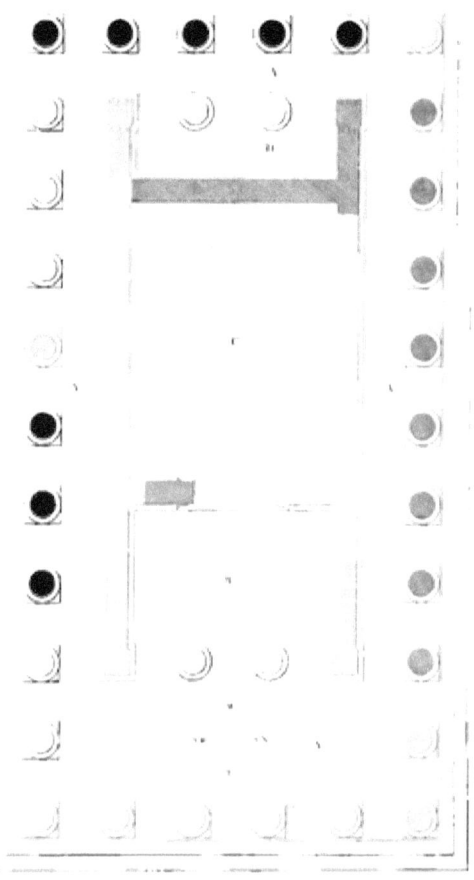

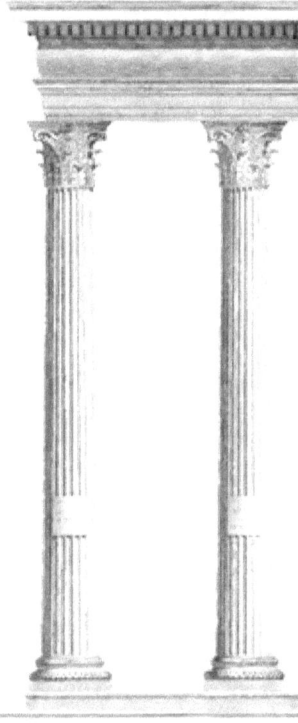

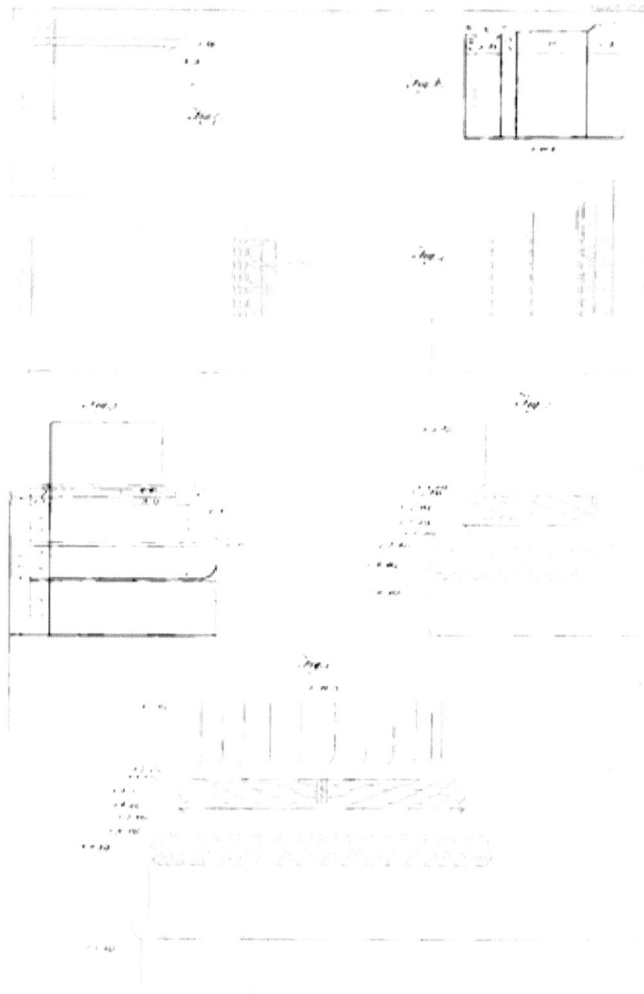

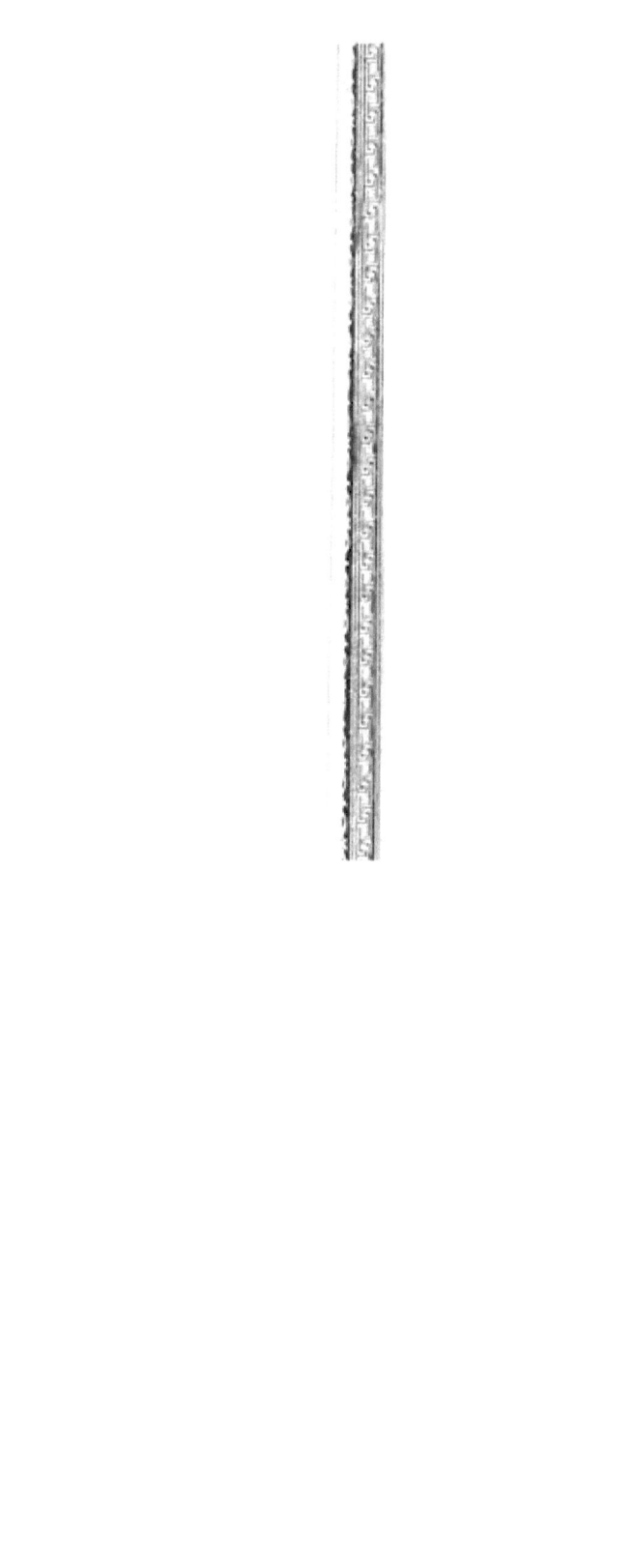

CHAPTER V.

SAMOS.

The island of Samos, notwithstanding its magnitude and importance, has been little visited by modern travellers, and its geography is in consequence so little understood, that in the year 1829, a map of its ancient capital was engraved at Paris, which represented the Heræum as situated within the walls of the city; while the English charts published previously to the Dilettanti mission were so faulty, that it was found impossible to correct them. The present survey of the ancient Samos contains only that part of the island immediately connected with the ancient city and the Heræum. The rest of the island, except the eastern coast, yet remains unexplored; and the inhabitants mentioned ruins in the interior which seem to be as yet unexamined. There are eighteen towns or large villages, and about as many hamlets in the island, the population of which may amount to about fifty thousand souls.

Samos lies between the parallels of latitude 37° 37′ and 37° 56′, and the longitude of the ancient city is about 27° east from London. The length of the island from east to west is about twenty-six miles. The town of Bathy or Vathi is situated at the extremity of a deep inlet, on the north-eastern side of the island, and this affords a safe anchorage for the vessels which visit the place annually for wine. A small mole, to protect the port from the north, would render it an excellent station. Bathy seems at present the most populous place, though not considered the capital of the island. On the shore are the houses of some of the merchants, with their magazines, and some of the agents or vice consuls of foreign states live near the beach. The habitations cover the northern side of a conical hill, and are approached by steep, crooked and dirty streets, scarcely possible on horseback.

Bathy may be about forty miles south of Smyrna, and seventeen from the opposite cape called Hypsile Boreum. Though surrounded by hills, the two peaked summits of Mount Mycale, now called Karene, on the continent of Asia, form the principal feature of the entrance of the port. Homer applies to this mountain the epithet ἀκριτόφυλλος.* Not far from Bathy, on the road to the ports in the streiglas or boccas of Samos, is the village of Palaio Kastro, where, notwithstanding the name, there do not appear any traces of antiquity. The ancient capital of the island can only be visited from Bathy by a very rugged path, from which, after an ascent of one hour, Mount Mycale is seen on the left, the ancient citadel in the centre, and the sole remaining column of the temple of Juno on the right, upon the southern coast of the island. After descending from this summit into the valley of Metelinous, and crossing a pretty and permanent stream, fringed with rhododaphne or oleanders, the village of Metelinous presents itself. This village has nine churches, and the inhabitants are said to possess most of the cultivable territory near the ancient city. Many fragments of sculpture, both in bronze and marble, are found in the vicinity. At a short distance from Metelinous, and separated from it by a low ridge of hills, stands the capital of Samos, now called, from that circumstance, Chora or "the City." The way to it lies through a pretty glen, watered by a perennial stream, called *Meseli Nero*, which rises under the mountain Vorliotes or Bouliotis. This city contains at present about three hundred houses, and is the residence of the Vaivode or governor, as well as of a cadi and the bishop: the last has a commodious residence in the town. At the period of the Dilettanti mission the Vaivode was a German renegado, who seemed well disposed, but was himself evidently governed by the Greek archons of the island. The mission having waited upon him, he returned the visit on the following morning at the Heræum, bringing a lamb as a present, and attended by one of the primates.

South of Chora lies a rich plain of considerable extent, which must anciently have supplied the city of Samos with provisions, and which is represented in the map accompanying this memoir. A high tower, which serves as a metochi to the monastery of Patmos, is visible near the coast, and might serve to guide a stranger to the Heræum. The remaining column of the temple of Juno may however be discovered from all parts of the plain. The mission was induced to lodge in some magazines on the shore, distant about fifty minutes from Chora, on account of their proximity to the ruins. These magazines were then newly erected, and had caused the destruction of the greater part of the remaining marbles of the temple of Juno, as was evident from the number of fragments, particularly of the bases, which appeared in the walls. This marble is white, with veins of blue or grey, and is found on the eastern coast of the island. Close to the magazines on the beach is a fountain, probably that which anciently supplied the temple. The river Imbrasos,

* Il. II. 869.

the favourite haunt of the goddess, flows at the distance of seven hundred yards to the west of the temple. Its banks are, as in ancient times, beautifully fringed with broom, oleander, and agnus castus, the plant dedicated to Juno which, here and at Chora, is rather a tree than a shrub. On the mountain Vatfiotes, west of the plain, and ending in the Cape Eis Ampelo, or Sampoulo, the ancient Ampelos, is the village of Baionda, containing about three hundred houses. Beyond is a plain, in which is a village, Marathro Campo, where ruins are said to exist. Above this is the lofty mountain Kerke, the ancient Cercetius, or Kerketeus of Strabo. Above the plain of Chora is the large and hospitable monastery of Stauro, or the Holy Cross. The Imbrasus could scarcely be called a running stream at its mouth in the month of June, though one branch from the village of Pyrgo is perennial. At no great distance from the shore, and below the village of Baionda, pronounced Vaionda, is a source of the Imbrasus, called Nero Trouvio, or the Water Hole. Nothing can exceed the beauty of the spot, or of the surrounding country; but the water is said to fail in July, August and September. The inhabitants have nevertheless an idea that the temple was supplied from this source. Near it, but upon a higher level, is an arcade, which the natives call an aqueduct, but which has more the appearance of a ruined church. On the mountain of Baionda is seen the monastery of the Agios Taxiarchos. Not far distant is that of the Megale Panagia.

The site of the Heræum, or temple of Juno, was probably in ancient times a swamp, and was approached by a causeway, such spots being often selected in Ionia, either from the real or imaginary security which they afforded against earthquakes. The temples of Diana at Ephesus, and Minerva Leucophryne at Magnesia ad Mæandrum, are examples of this choice. Vitruvius speaks of the foundations of such edifices; but if we might judge of the real effect of the marsh upon the durability of the edifices, from the comparison of those ruins which remain, with others founded upon rocks, we might perhaps find that the only difference consists in the circumstance, that the temples situated in swamps seem to have been overthrown by a simultaneous motion like a wave, in consequence of which the columns have been thrown down in parallel lines in the direction of the shock, while the others have tottered and fallen nearly on the spot, as at the temple of Minerva-Polias at Priene. The temple of Juno was raised upon a platform, to which there was an ascent of several steps. The columns still existing are so widely separated, and their diameters of such different magnitudes, as lead us to conjecture that the pure ancient temple was surrounded by a portico of later date. Herodotus mentions three magnificent works of the Samians; the temple, however, excelling the others in magnificence and extent. Rhoecus, the son of Phileus, was the architect of this celebrated structure. There was in all probability a propylæum to the Heræum, of which the Doric fragments are yet visible. The statue of Juno, which ornamented the temple of Samos, was of bronze, and existed till about the year 1260 after Christ in the square of Constantine at Constantinople. Nicetas Choniates, the Byzantine historian, relates, in a fragment preserved by Fabricius, that this magnificent work of art was thrown down by the crusaders during the pillage of that city, and that the head alone, when broken off, was of such a prodigious weight, that eight oxen could with difficulty drag it to the palace, where it was melted with the other fragments of the statue into staters,* and employed in all probability in paying the Venetians for the transport of the troops. Near the temple was found a small statue of brass, which the labourer who discovered it filed in a barbarous manner, in order to ascertain whether it was of gold. It is now in the possession of the Rev. G. A. Browne of Trinity College, Cambridge, and is probably an exact representation of the great statue of Juno.†

PLATE I.

MAP OF THE COUNTRY AROUND SAMOS.

It appears from an examination of the district, that there was anciently a magnificent road from the Heræum to the city of Samos, which we may safely conclude was termed the Sacred Way, and to have been the usual approach of the processions to the shrine of the goddess. The map shews the position of several heaps or tumuli which once decorated this Way; but whether they were barrows, or the sites of magnificent tombs, cannot now be ascertained without excavation. The distance between the Heræum and the city of Samos is about four thousand five hundred yards, passing at five hundred paces a stream, and at eight hundred and sixty another river and marsh. At one thousand and twenty-five paces one of the most remarkable tumuli is near on the left. At one thousand six hundred and fifty paces is a modern custom-house on the beach; at two thousand two hundred and fifty-five is a mill; and at two thousand seven hundred and fifty are the walls of the ancient Samos, which run up to the summit of the rocky hill on the left. Near the road are seen sarcophagi decorated with festoons, and a fine source of salt water. On entering the old city, are some modern ruins, now called Odontia, or the teeth, from their form. Following the course of the walls and towers up the ascent on the left, the citadel is seen covering the summit of the hill. The walls are all constructed in horizontal courses, and vary in thickness from nine to fourteen feet. In some places the projecting cornice yet remains, and even the lower courses of the battlements. Five gates may be traced upon the summit, but it would be difficult to imagine their use, as they generally open upon rocks and precipices.‡ From the fortress may be seen a

---

* Lib. 21. c. 60.

† Note the temple was also found the brazen head of a griffin, which may have been one of those which, according to Herodotus, B. iv. 152, surrounded a large votive vase of brass, dedicated by the Samians to the temple of Juno. This is now in the possession of R. P. Knight, Esq.

In the walls near the Heræum are many fragments of statues. The thighs, an arm, and a foot of a female figure, of Parian marble, originally about twelve feet in height, lie in a neighbouring field. Near the temple are also pieces of sculpture in basso relievo, the figures of which have evidently been larger than those of the Parthenon. It is proper to state, for the information of future travellers, that the ruins of the great temple will soon, in all probability, become a quarry, from whose materials will be taken for the construction of a village on the shore; and if so, much may be discovered that the mission in 1812 were not enabled to examine. By the contrivance of Pisani, the interpreter at Constantinople, the island of Samos was not mentioned in the firman, but the names of Scyppo and Hieskelir substituted. The consequence was, that the archons of the island prohibited the people from working at the excavations, and the great bowers of the mission were obliged, in the month of June, to work themselves with spades and pickaxes, while their interpreter was employed in drawing off the inhabitants from the spot, by telling them amusing stories, and the practice of several ridiculous mummeries.

‡ The towers are usually about four feet in thickness, in two perpendicular courses. One well preserved, on the west, has two long holes on the west, two on the south, and one on the north, with a door on the east. These apertures diminish toward the outer face in the proportion of two feet to ten inches.

glen, in which are the remains of an aqueduct. This glen separates the citadel from the neighbouring mountains, and at its north-eastern extremity is the church of St. John or Agiani, where may be traced the entrance of that subterraneous canal, by which the water of a beautiful source near the present church was conducted under the mountain to the city of Samos. Near the fountain is also the church of St. George, and the capital of a Doric column, the abacus of which is two feet square. This canal is another of the great undertakings of the Samians recorded by the historian. On the southern side of the hill, and not far from the ancient theatre of Samos, is a cavern with a small metochi, and this cavern is said to have some connection with the subterraneous aqueduct. If it communicates with it, it must probably be by a shaft, for the level seems too high for the source at Agiani, though this circumstance has not been ascertained. There is a subterraneous channel near the head of the great mole, at Port Tigani, which might be, with more probability, taken for the spot to which the water from Agiani was conducted. The theatre is excavated in the side of the hill, overlooking the sea, and some of the seats yet remain. The diameter is about two hundred and forty-six feet. From the top of the hill the ancient mole, one of the wonders of Samos, may be seen in the sea, though little of its superstructure remains. The great depth of the water must have added much to the difficulty of constructing it.[*] It is much to be doubted whether the mole was ever two stadia in length, but it is nevertheless a stupendous work. The ruins of several edifices may yet be discovered near the sea, and among others the remains of a Corinthian portico.

In the eastern wall is seen a little gate, nearly perfect, and of curious construction. There was probably another gate near the sea. To the east of the old city lies a plain called Miso Campo, or Meso Goupo; and more distant is a promontory, called Pyliámou, or Hypsile, with a rocky islet. On the right of this is the Cape Trogyllion, which is the point of Mount Mycale, on the continent of Asia, and forms the entrance to the streights or boccas of Samos. Near the cape is a port, where Saint Paul anchored, now the resort of privateers and corsairs, and called the Port of the Panagia, or Holy Virgin. Above it, the natives say, is a monastery of Saint Paul. On the cape, eastward of Pyliámou, called Koukoura, is a circular peribolus, of grey marble. It is now almost buried by loose stones, but the masonry appears ancient. The diameter seems to have been about eighty-seven feet. There is another ruin on the next cape, which is called Grza Poulia; and between the two is a bay, called Merjik, and by the Greeks Klima, probably on account of a bad road, up steps, cut in the rock, leading into the interior. The first peribolus is probably the site of the ancient Potidium of Samos.

Beyond Grza Poulia is a port called Mollah Ibrahim, from which there is a road, or path, to Palaio Kastro and Bathy, through a wild and beautiful pass in the mountains. The opposite coast of Mycale is magnificent, and finely wooded. There is no appearance of any population; nor indeed could the Panionium have been placed in any convenient spot on this side the mountain, except at Changli, unless ruins should be found to exist near the port at Trogyllion. The

[*] Herodotus.

little island now called Agio Nicolo, the ancient Narthex, lies nearly central in the channel. There are two other small rocks in the boccas. There are many inscriptions in the island; one of which, consisting of ten verses, alternately hexameters and pentameters, was on so thin a slab of marble, and so perfect, that it was brought away by the Dilettanti mission, and presented to the University of Cambridge, through the Earl of Hardwicke.

PLATE II.

VIEW OF THE REMAINS OF THE TEMPLE.

Several of the bases of the columns are remaining in their places; but, for the most part, so dispersed and distant one from the other, that it is impossible to form any satisfactory idea of the original plan. Like the temple of Apollo Didymæus, and that of Jupiter Olympius at Athens, this appears to have been a decastyle and dipteral temple, and, like the former, to have had twenty-one columns in the sides or flanks.

As near as it was possible to obtain distances on ground so broken and encumbered, two columns in the second row of the principal front, were one hundred and six feet apart; and on supposition that five columns were intermediately situated, we shall have an average distance of 17′. 8″.2 between the axes of two adjoining columns.

The whole extent of the temple in the flanks appears to have been three hundred and forty-four feet, and in front one hundred and sixty-six.

The lower part of one of the bases of the columns still remains in its position at the north-east angle of the temple.

The diameter of the columns belonging to the outer peristyle is 6′.5″.4.

PLATE III.

THE BASE AND THE UPPER PART OF THE SHAFT OF ONE OF THE COLUMNS.

The base is of very singular construction, without the lower torus.

PLATE IV.

DETAILS OF THE COLUMNS.

Fig. 1. Section through the echinus of the capital.
Fig. 2. Section through the ovalo.
Fig. 3. Horizontal section of the echinus.
Fig. 4. Elevation of the same.
Fig. 5. Fragments of volutes found amongst the ruins.
  A. Section.
  B. Elevation.
Fig. 6. Base of the column at the north east angle, shewing the section of the steps.

PLATE V.

SECTIONS THROUGH THE MOULDINGS FORMING THE BASES OF THE COLUMNS.

A great variety in the mouldings is observable in both the exterior and interior ranges.

PLATE VI.

FRAGMENTS FOUND AMONGST THE RUINS.

Fig. 1, 2, 3. Details of an ornamented moulding.
Fig. 4. The capital of a small Ionic column. The canal of the volute, instead of being hollow, or sunk, is here raised.
Fig. 5. Section across the volute.
Fig. 6. The capital of a Doric column.
Fig. 7. Section of the annulets.

PLATE VII.

ORDER AT LARGE OF A DORIC BUILDING.

About the centre of the ancient city and not far from the sea, are considerable remains of a portico or agora. Its site is marked in the map by the words " ancient ruins."

The style of architecture is manifestly Roman. The cymatium of the capital is without a band or fillet.

The pedestal with the base, probably of an Ionic column, is one of several belonging to the same building.

PLATE VIII.

FRAGMENTS FOUND AT SAMOS.

In the map a spot is indicated, where some ruins of a Corinthian building were discovered. The cornice, and the angle of a pediment, with encircled mouldings, were found amongst them. It is of white marble.

The shadowed cornice, of which we have also given an outline drawn to a larger scale, forms the lintel over the window of a small chapel above the theatre, a little to the east. It is in the immediate neighbourhood of the large cavern, containing a reservoir of water, supplied by two springs, which has already been mentioned.

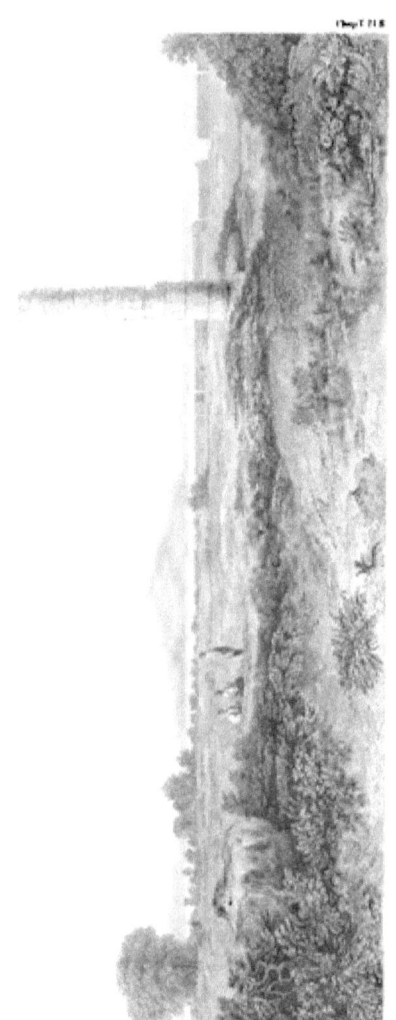

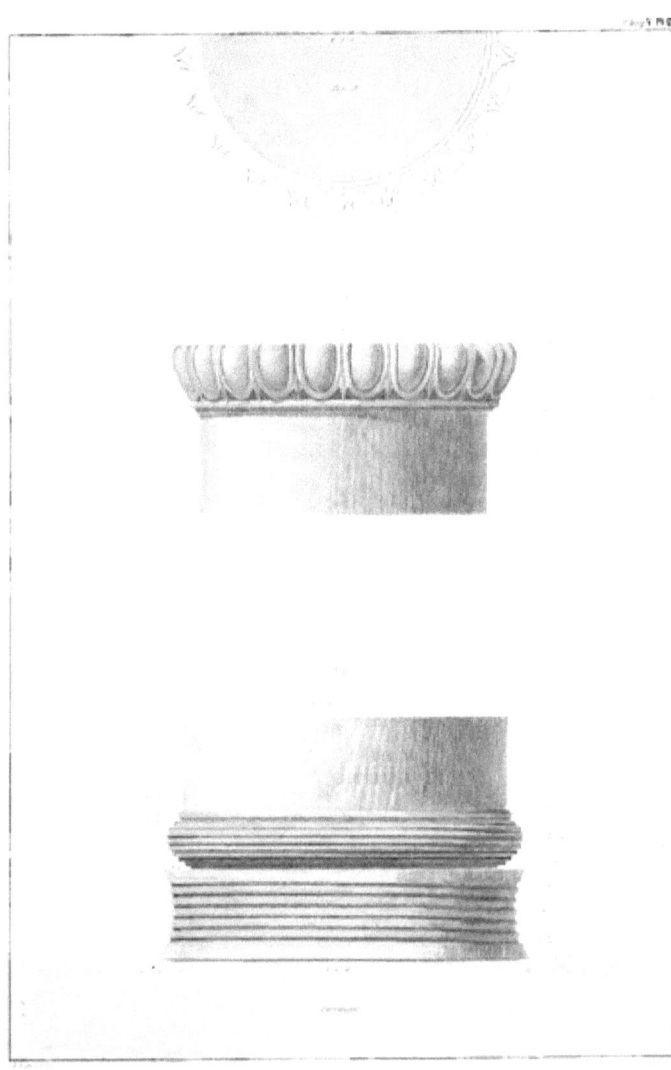

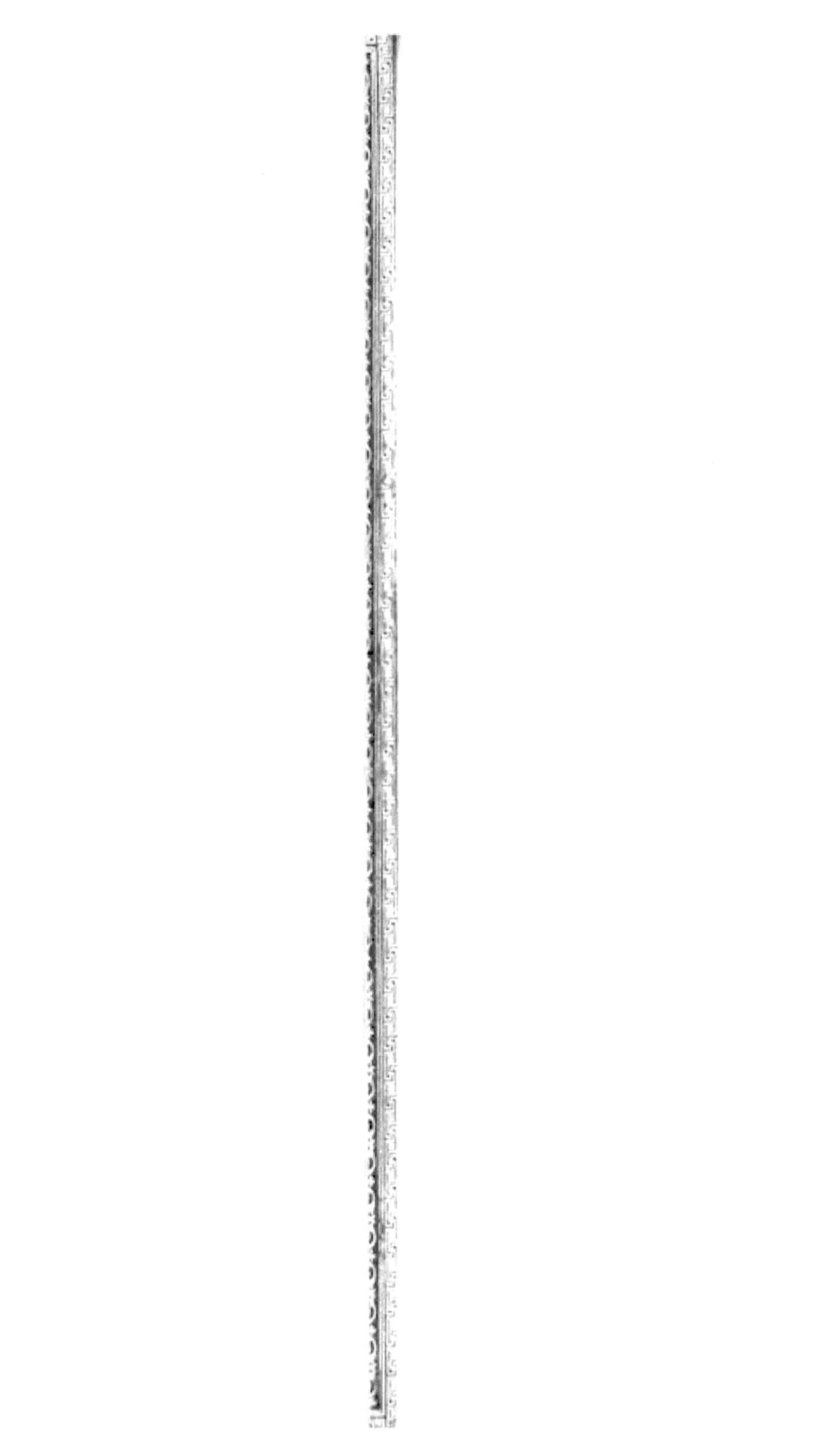

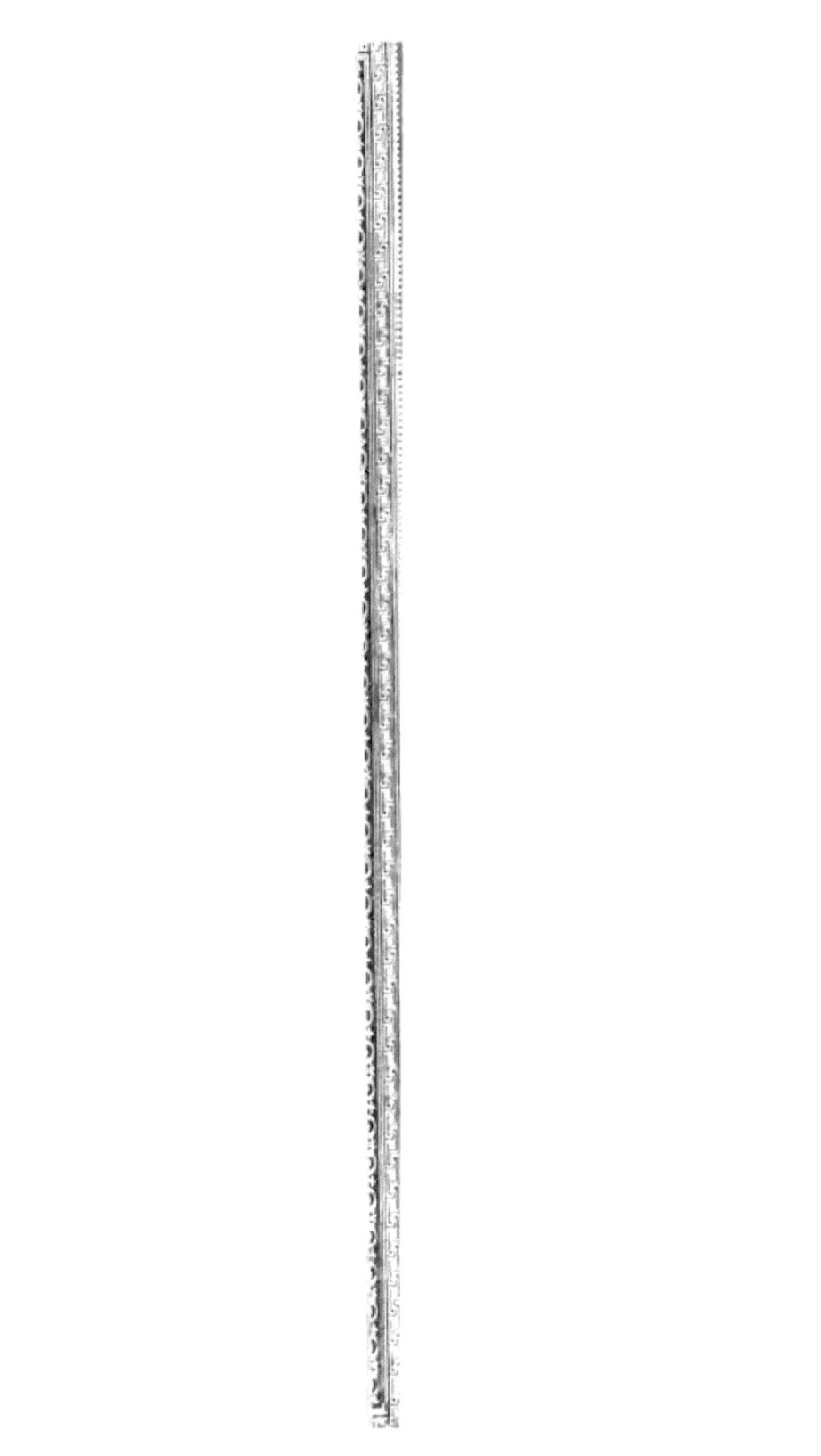

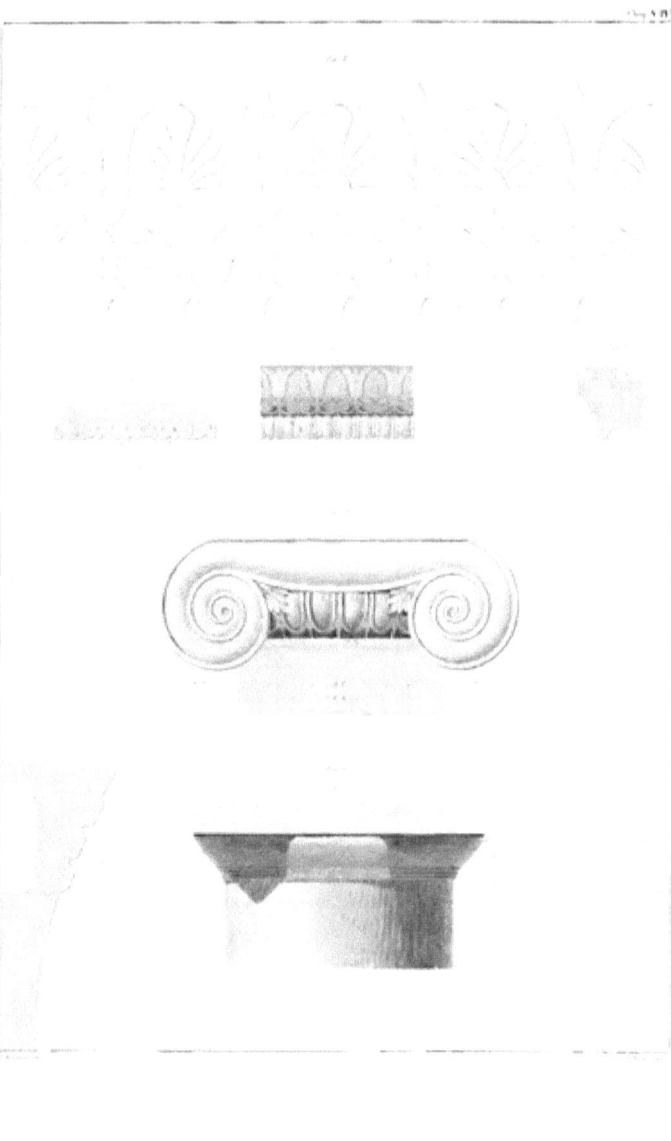

www.ingramcontent.com/pod-product-compliance
Lightning Source LLC
Chambersburg PA
CBHW020756230426
43666CB00007B/722